I0459881

HAPPY SOXX

Cancer hates Color

A man's journey fighting cancer with humor
Stress relieving humor in the face of cancer

Mac Churchill

Copyright © 2025 by Mac Churchill

ISBN: 979-8-88615-264-7 (Paperback)

All rights reserved. No part of this publication may be reproduced, distributed, or transmitted in any form or by any means, including photocopying, recording, or other electronic or mechanical methods, without the prior written permission of the publisher, except in the case brief quotations embodied in critical reviews and other noncommercial uses permitted by copyright law.

The views expressed in this book are solely those of the author and do not necessarily reflect the views of the publisher, and the publisher hereby disclaims any responsibility for them.

Inks and Bindings
888-290-5218
www.inksandbindings.com
orders@inksandbindings.com

Contents

Foreword

By Lu Jo Churchill

I married The Energizer Bunny. He had boundless energy and did everything on five hours of sleep a night! Even after being diagnosed with a rare form of cancer, Myelodysplastic Syndrome, he still ran a successful business, served on three or four charitable civic and business boards at a time. He worked out with a trainer three times a week, went to a weekly breakfast club once a week, and a luncheon group once a month. He played golf once a week, and we rarely missed a party. We hosted many civic and charitable parties. We traveled the world!

From the time of his diagnosis in January 2014, his health and energy spiraled downward through chemotherapy, a clinical trial at M.D. Anderson in Houston and finally to a Bone Marrow Transplant at UTSW in Dallas in 2019. The recovery time for that is over a two-year period involving weekly return trips to monitor the colonization of the new marrow cells.

In late 2021, he accidentally scraped the top of his head. A month later, the injured area had grown larger and was beginning to darken. It was a squamous cell cancer that rapidly grew to a 3" X 4" mass, which was removed by a MOHS surgeon in January 2022. She removed the involved tissue, which extended to the cranial bone. The bone then had to be covered by skin from the back of his neck.

By March, my husband was having shooting pain in his left ear. Nothing showed up in PET scans, CT scans, or Ultrasound tests until May. Cancer was spreading from his earlier head wound to the left side of his face. A team of four surgeons performed a twelve-hour surgery to remove most of his left ear, the ear canal, adjacent lymph nodes, the carotid artery, and some of the trapezius muscle from his left shoulder and the nerve that operates muscles on the left side of his face.

His carotid artery was replaced by the saphenous vein from his left leg. That incision went from his groin to his knee. This was followed by six and a half weeks of chemotherapy and radiation. Eight months later, cancer had moved to the right side of his face. This surgery was not as extensive as the previous one but required another six and a half weeks of chemotherapy and radiation.

Early in his diagnosis, he busied himself by forming a group of businessmen to complete a stalled bridge project that led into downtown. He continued his usual meetings and made sure that friends who needed emotional support during their difficult times had him to talk with or just meet for coffee. He wants to bring smiles and hope to everyone around him.

We cherish his doctors, nurses, technicians, and staff at UTSW and each of the clinics who treated us as they would treat their own families. Here are some of his stories. Hopefully, they will make you smile too!

Chapter 1
A Positive Spirit

I want to share the method that I have been able to employ while coping with the intense stress and pain in my journey of fighting cancer. This journey includes both the patients and treatment providers. I am not a licensed therapist, just a guy trying to cope with the disease.

Living your life-fighting cancer is grueling and can be filled with more downs than ups. The caregivers face the same grueling experience with each patient. The goal is a Cure. The path requires a determined, focused, and Positive Spirit Attitude.

The secret ingredient to this Positive Spirit was coupling it with humor. This is my coping method, and it may not work for anyone else, but it has kept me able to see the path ahead.

The humor was spontaneous and not meant to do anything more than create momentary relief from the fight. My method evolved over a period of years. The first couple of years, I was in denial even though I was taking chemotherapy. One day, I was waiting my turn to see the doctor. I was fully focused on myself. I looked up and around the waiting room. I noticed that everyone was wearing gray or black. That was so depressing to me. I decided from that moment on I was not going to dwell in the negative world.

I began slowly by wearing colored shirts, no dark colors. This was the first volley in my fight against cancer. Later, I added colored soxx. I called them Happy Soxx. These daily depression-resistant displays made me feel better. Eventually, it evolved into Hawaiian shirts, colorful soxx, and shoes.

The humor side of my coping developed slowly. The humor I used was mainly with the caregivers. Most caregivers are treated more like necessary evils. Quite the opposite is true. Most caregivers are very caring by their nature and have a thick protective shell. This shell allows them to deal with the daily stress cancer poses.

Using humor to cope with cancer is a brave choice that can really boost your mood and help you get through your diagnosis and treatment. The humor I tried to communicate was never said in a derogatory, mean, or silly clownish fashion. The humor seemed to work better if it was delivered with a straight face. The target had to consider if I was serious- think about it- and quickly realize I was only kidding.

My experience showed that the doctors were the hardest ones to make smile.

I believe that is because they are operating in one "Life or Death decision" after another. Although, I did have a doctor assure me everything was going to be all right because: "He stayed at a Holiday Inn Express last night."

That made me relax and chuckle, too! Somebody beat me at my own game. One of Jimmy Buffet's songs so aptly puts it, "If we couldn't laugh, we would all go insane!"

I have found in life that people judge you by how you make them feel. It only takes a little extra effort to find out the shuttle driver's name, the receptionist, the technician, the nurse, and you get the idea. I have found out the best way to remember their names is by word association or fun nicknames. I wanted them to feel good about themselves and the vital jobs they were doing! I wanted to complement them! A smile, a chuckle, or a laugh can make people feel good.

Using their name makes them feel like they are important, and they want to take extra good care of you. Napoleon Hill, in his timeless book "Think and Grow Rich," basically said that for everything that happens, there is a "seed of good." Now, that seed of good might be the size of a mustard seed or an example of what not to do. We learn from our disappointments and learn not to repeat mistakes. A Positive Spirit can be developed by searching for that "seed of good" in everything we do.

My illness has allowed me to focus more on my family. My work had always consumed my days and nights. Sure, I was the father attending all my kids' events at school and athletics. I was there for all the special occasions and family trips.

My real focus was to be the breadwinner and to work to improve my family's standard of living. Now, all that has changed. I have time to think about my wife, children, bonus children, and grandchildren. I have time to be a Positive Spirit in their lives.

I have found that having a Positive Outlook or Spirit helps you in everything you do. I think that it is especially true in your fight against cancer. Every caregiver I have asked about this Positive Spirit enthusiastically agrees with me.

So, don't give up the fight.

They are finding cures for medical problems every day. We just have to hang around long enough for them to find a cure.

Chapter 2
Golf Cart Wheelie

When making the tour of cancer doctors, transfusions, and infusions at MD Anderson in Houston, the patients must get to offices and clinics that are in other buildings. Healthy people find the walk good exercise, but patients are often challenged and weak. The hospital provides a shuttle service between buildings that are connected by skywalks. One regular destination was one mile from where I would check-in for a blood draw then begin scheduled appointments. Several appointments were a long distance apart. There were many days when my first appointment began at 7 AM, and we left the hospital complex at 11 PM.

Shuttle vehicles are extended golf carts and can carry six to eight passengers. There is a loading area where the patients gather to be transferred to the next building.

I found a seat right behind the driver. We took off at a slow pace, down the long hall to our next appointment.

Recognizing that most patients don't acknowledge the shuttle driver, I asked, "So, what's your name?"

"James," he said.

"How long have you been driving, James?"

"Six years now."

"I bet you have met some real characters in your six years."

"I sure have!"

"Have you driven any celebrities?"

"Oh sure, more often than you might think."

"Have you ever done a wheelie on this golf cart?"

"Heavens, No!"

We arrived at the destination building.

"Thanks for driving us. It has been a pleasure to ride with you," I said.

We made our scheduled appointments and returned to catch the shuttle after completing that day's procedures.

"Hey, James, can we catch a ride with you?"

"Sure, hop on!"

"James, are you going to do a wheelie like the last time we rode with you?" All of this was said just loud enough to be overheard by my fellow passengers. Everyone who overheard the conversation was straining to hear his reply.

"Awh, you know this shuttle couldn't get off the ground with a rocket booster!"

He was 100% correct, but the banter was fun, and patients were briefly asking themselves if this golf cart could really do a wheelie with eight people on it. I did notice that everyone held a secure grip on the shuttle. And for a moment, it took their minds off of their illnesses.

Upon arrival, everyone let out a little sigh of relief. Most had a small smile, and they all thanked James for the ride (even if it was without a wheelie or a "Thank You for not doing a wheelie.")

James was standing beside his shuttle with a smile and proud of the fact everyone had recognized him with a thank you. A shuttle cart driver can be a thankless job, but not today. James's proud smile was my reward as we walked away to our next appointment.

Chapter 3
Leprosy Exam

Three years of various Chemotherapy drugs had come to an unsuccessful end. Cancer was winning the war. I returned to MD Anderson after ten months in the Clinical Trial. The pharmaceutical company that was testing a potential drug used in the clinical trial went bankrupt. This even limited my options.

When I sat down with my doctor to discuss the situation, he pointed towards a bone marrow transplant. A bone marrow transplant is a surgery with many risks. The mortality rate not so long ago was as high as 20%. Those odds are worse than Russian Roulette. The rates today are below 4%. There are a number of factors that figure into your chances of survival:

Number 1: Your age. Transplants are rarely performed after age 70. Your other health issues and complications may make you ineligible.

Number 2: Donor availability or a match to your genetic profile.

Number 3: Available caregiver for at least a year.

After discussing options with my doctor (there were no other options), we decided to begin the tests that would determine transplant eligibility. I was sent to a doctor in the transplant department, who agreed to see me immediately. The Doctor's nurse told me to have a seat. She began a battery of routine questions while the doctor reviewed my medical history.

My chemotherapy doctor had called ahead and explained my treatment history. The transplant doctor took over and asked some of his own routine questions. Then he asked me to step up onto the examination table. He began the exam by pressing on my stomach. Reaching under my sweater, he asked, "Do you have aches or pains?

"No, sir!"

"Do you have any sores or rashes?"

"No, sir, just this mild case of Leprosy." Of course, I didn't really have Leprosy. I was just teasing.

He jerked his hands back, spun on his heels, and immediately began washing his hands. The nurse also took several steps back. It seemed to dawn on him what had just really happened. He looked back over his shoulder with a slight smile and said, "You got me on that one!"

The doctor was a good sport and did approve me for a Bone Marrow transplant.

This was my first effort to add humor to my Cancer treatment. Admittedly, it was pretty lame, but it opened the door.

I decided to have the surgery performed closer to home and opted for UT Southwestern in Dallas.

Chapter 4

Happy Soxx

When going through the Cancer Treatment process, you become very familiar with the waiting room. Patients are looking around the room at each other. All are wondering what the other person is experiencing. A few look to be in worse shape than others. Everyone there is thinking about survival. We are all praying that the doctor has good news and that our "numbers" have improved.

Being a cancer patient, you typically see multiple doctors depending on your cancer type and location. I was diagnosed with Myelodysplastic Syndrome, so I saw:

A General Practitioner
A Radiologist
A Dermatologist
A Hematology Oncologist
A Transplant Surgeon
A Cardiologist
A Mohs Surgeon
A Cosmetic Reconstruction Surgeon
A Head and Neck Surgeon
A Chemotherapist
A Neurologist
An Infectious Disease Specialist
A Dentist and A Nutritionist

All of these doctors have their own waiting rooms, and many are at different hospitals and in different cities. All reception/check-in processes are the same. You are asked your name and date of birth. You usually begin the journey whispering your name so that the others in the waiting room can't hear you. You still don't want anyone to know that you have cancer, and you still don't believe it yourself.

The first couple of years of treatment, I went from one waiting room to the next. I found myself withdrawn and focused on my illness, the blood cancer known as MDS. Looking up from my chair, I began to notice a certain pattern of dress in the waiting room. Everyone seemed to be wearing Black or Gray clothes.

Naturally, everyone is inwardly focused, and darker colors allow them to blend in with others in the waiting room. This common blending was perceived by me as depressing. I decided to escape the depression trap. I began by wearing colored shirts. I wanted to wear colors that might lift my spirits and others around me. Not clown color and not anything with a message on it. I just wanted the colors to be a sign of Hope and Resolve to fight cancer and even win the battle.

The first to notice were the nurses, assistants, and then the doctors. I was in close contact with all of them as my treatment progressed. Many favorable comments were made, especially after I explained my Positive Spirit reasoning. They seemed to look forward to my next visit to see what I might be wearing at our next appointment. Over time, I added some Hawaiian shirts. These Hawaiian shirts had the added benefit of taking me back to my trips to Hawaii. I could remember the beautiful beaches, relaxing waves rolling in, lush tropical islands, and bright sunny days.

I never wanted to make light of anyone's condition or act like our situations weren't serious, I only wanted people to perhaps think about happier times in their lives.

Later, I added colorful, comfortable soxx and shoes. The shoes I chose were Swims brand in Aqua or Orange. These shoes were colorful loafers made of rubber and mesh and designed to be worn around a pool or on the beach. These brought many comments and smiles. My ultimate goal was to be a Positive Spirit to those I was around.

I decided to come out of this journey Better than I went into it.

When I arrived at the Dentist's office to resume my routine checkups, I received a warm welcome back. It was good to see familiar faces. My transplant doctors had not wanted me to have dental exams that could expose me to bacterial infections.

Immediately after I sat down, the dental hygienist noticed my multi-colored soxx.

"Are those your Happy Soxx?"

"They sure are! Aren't they fun?"

"You know I try to wear Happy Soxx. Yes, I even have some on today," she said.

"Oh, you have got to let me see them!"

Hidden under her dark blue scrubs were her Happy Soxx!

"These are Johnny Cash soxx. They have his prison picture on them," she proudly announced.

Well, you could have knocked me over with a feather. I don't know what I was expecting, but Johnny Cash in prison was not on the list. We had a good laugh, and she began cleaning my teeth. Even the dentist visit can be less painful when two Positive Spirits meet.

One pre-surgery nurse had on a pair of neon green athletic shoes. "Do you have to plug those in at night?" I asked her jokingly.

She smiled and said, "Heck no, these don't glow in the dark. You know I have to wear dark blue scrubs to work every day, and it's kind of depressing.

These are my happy shoes. They make me feel happy when I put them on."

I was inwardly rejoicing that I had found a kindred spirit and said, "I do the same thing. I am wearing this bright blue sweater for the same reason. Check these soxx out. Yes, they had Hawaiian palm trees and orange fish all over them. I guess we are Happy Rebels against a world of black and gray." Hooray for Happy!

The rebel in you can come out in many forms. The fight against cancer can be as small as "Happy Soxx" or as outrageous as a Yodeling Pickle Choir.

So every day when you get up — smile as you put on your Happy Soxx. You are joining the army of positive spirts and prayers fighting against cancer.

Chapter 5

COVID Testing

During the COVID pandemic, hospitals were required to institute all kinds of protocols.

One check-in, I had a lot of fun with was a mask requirement and temperature check as you entered the hospital. It went something like this:

When anyone entered the hospital or any medical facility, there would be a white plastic folding table manned by one or two attendants. A line would usually form to wait while they checked visitors and patients for masks, and they swiped your forehead for your temperature. Well, when it became my time in line, I would jump back and ask, "You're not going to do like that nurse did yesterday taking my temperature, are you?"

"What do you mean?"

Looking around to make sure no children were around and a few patients were listening, I said, "Well, when it came time to take my temperature—she made me drop my pants, and she swiped my butt with a thermometer!"

"No, she didn't, No, she didn't — oh, you're kidding! Ha Ha Hah"

Everyone in line is in a different degree of pain or stress. They gave a controlled giggle or just shook their heads and smiled.

My mission was accomplished! Even a moment of stress relief during cancer treatment is welcome, and it brought a smile to my face to watch their reactions.

Then, it was time for the pre-exam by the doctor's tech in her office.

"That's a pretty unusual protocol to check for COVID downstairs," I said.

"What do you mean? What happened?"

"Well, normally, when you check in downstairs, they check you for your mask and swipe your forehead for your temperature."

"That's right."

"Well, not today! When it became my turn in line, she made me drop my pants, and she swiped my butt!"

Taking a moment to evaluate, she broke out in a laugh!

Then, there was a nurse updating my medical records at a later appointment. She asked all of the usual questions and then asked, "How is your appetite?"

"No problem there,"

"Are you having any anxiety?"

"Why, yes."

"Tell me about it."

"Well, you know when you check in downstairs?"

"Yes," she thinks there could be all kinds of issues with anger or a patient misunderstanding the necessity of the new procedures.

Well, the girls that check for a mask and take your temperature downstairs made me drop my pants and swiped my butt!"

"No way! Ha Ha Hah, I get it. That would make me anxious, too!"

Later, at the dermatologist's office, I had an early morning appointment after the COVID pandemic had subsided. We were led back to the exam room, and on arrival, I asked the nurse!

"When did they reinstate the COVID protocols?"

"What?"

"Well, remember during the COVID pandemic, they had a table by the entrance where they would check to make sure everyone who entered the building had a mask on and would check their temperature? Just now, when we came in, they checked for masks, and then they made me drop my pants and swiped my butt with a thermometer!"

"They did what! Who did that? Oh, you're kidding." He was bent over laughing!

"Now that's funny. That's the way to start the day off," He was still laughing.

Humor can be a powerful tool for coping with difficult emotions. We sometimes forget that those treating us are dealing with stress all day. A little humor relieves stress and is good medicine for the patient and caregiver.

Chapter 6
Senior Pole Vaulting

One time, I needed to change an upcoming doctor's appointment. I would rarely change appointments because my health comes first unless it was my grandkids who were always first for my attention!

So, I called and requested a change. I told the appointment scheduler that the appointment conflicted with my Senior Pole-Vaulting tryouts. She worked with me, and we found a date that did not conflict.

The appointment day arrived. Upon entering the offices, I got a feeling that the nurses were watching me very cautiously like I was a suspect.

We were shown into the exam room, and the nurse's assistant began her battery of routine questions to update my records. The questions were all the same, except she seemed to expect a little more detail of recent events.

"Have you fallen lately? She asked while measuring my height and looking carefully at my head.

"No."

"Do you have any new sores or injuries?" she asked while looking very carefully from my fingertips to my shoulder as she put the blood pressure cuff on my arm.

I was a recovering Bone Marrow Transplant patient, so more thorough questions were very common.

"No."

"Have you taken Aspirin or Tylenol recently?"

"No, mam."

She almost seemed disappointed in my answers. What was that all about?

"I'll send the doctor in shortly," she said most professionally.

My Doctor arrived and reviewed the nurse's medical notes. She gave me a quick up and down. She then began to review my blood test results. The doctor seems a little more chatty than usual. "Let me check your ankles for swelling. Have you noticed any bruising anywhere?

"No, ma'am."

"So, I have just got to ask you. The office is divided on whether you really do pole vault or not.

Half of my staff thinks you are a pole vaulter, and the other half doesn't.

They have placed bets, and there is money riding on this! "

Wow! That explains the unusual feeling I was getting when I arrived today. They were all trying to get some inside information on how to place their bet!

"Heck no! I don't Pole Vault. I have switched to Bull Riding; it only lasts for 8 seconds!"

So half the staff was relieved, and the other half was disappointed. One nurse even asked my wife if she had any pictures of my athletic events! But we all had a good laugh!

Laughing is good for you both mentally and physically!

Chapter 7

Good Golly Miss Molly

Infusion rooms at hospitals are serious and quiet. When you need blood, this is where you go. You also go here when you need to have blood drawn (phlebotomy).

A blood transfusion usually takes 2 - 3 hours, depending on the amount needed. You are made comfortable in a reclining chair with pillows and warm blankets. The technicians draw your blood. They confirm your blood type and measure your blood counts (red blood cells, white blood cells, and platelets). This tells them how much blood to give or take. You are then "hooked up" to the IV.

During one of my treatments, I was visited by Molly. She was a ray of sunshine with a wagging tail. Actually, two volunteers were leading around a yellow lab to visit patients who were having infusions. Molly just happens to be the double of my dog at home. Infusions are lonely and boring, but Molly was welcomed with open arms.

"Molly, thank you for stopping by to visit with me."

Molly places her head on my free arm and looks up at me. I was feeling the love that dogs give unconditionally.

"Well, Molly, have you visited with quite a few other patients today?"

"You don't say. That's a lot! I know that you made them feel as special as I feel now. Your visit is extra special to me because I have a Lucy at home that you remind me of. Lucy comforts me at home. You would like to meet her. I'm sure that you have more stops on your love and comfort tour today. Please drop by when you are in the neighborhood. Thanks again for the visit. I hope to see you again soon."

These angel visits are extremely comforting and take the loneliness out of treatment time. No matter how caring the nurses or technicians are, it's hard to beat that instant unconditional love a dog brings. Thank you to the volunteers who take the time to share their Mollys with patients who are fighting cancer.

Chapter 8
Lieing Scales

When going through the journey of Cancer treatment, there are routine procedures. It seems like every doctor's office and every hospital has them. The first usually involves a preliminary medical exam. This is where they weigh you, take your blood pressure, temperature, check your oxygen level, check your pulse, and ask you if there are any changes in your medication or if you have had a fall since you were here last time.

The nurse's assistant went through the battery of questions and told me to step upon the scale.

"I can't do that!"

"Why not? It's not going to bite you, honey."

"You know those scales. They lie."

She issued a drill Sergeant order: "Get up there."

I stepped onto the scales and said, "See, I told you it lied! It says I weigh 185, and when I weighed this morning at home, it said I weighed 149."

She was obviously a seasoned veteran of the weigh-in wars and had heard this complaint before.

"All right, take off all your clothes, and we will weigh you again!" She was much too quick with the Perfect Response. She completely called my bluff! I wasn't about to really take off all of my clothes!

We all laughed and went on our way. All of us were a little less stressed. Later, at another doctor's office, I was asked to step up onto the scales. "You know these scales lie?" I said, questioning her directive.

"How do you figure that?" she asked in a tone of voice that sounded like she was dealing with a matter that was a waste of time.

"Well, when I weighed this morning at home, I weighed 149."

"OK, hop up on the scales, and let's see what it says," she said, shaking her head.

"See, I told you it lies! It says 186," I said quite confidently.

"You know, that's a funny thing about our scales. They point out more patients that need glasses than miss the weight calculation."

She let me know that she was onto me, and we all smiled.

Chapter 9

All State Pride

I have been a positive person my whole life. I had a strong mother who believed I could achieve anything that I tried. My mother never limited me or herself in what she thought could be accomplished. By the time I was in sixth grade, my mother had been divorced twice with three young boys to raise in the 1950s.

We moved several times to be near her job. It was then that I made the decision to either take the good or bad path in life. I wanted to succeed! These days, people blame everyone but themselves for their own bad choices. I certainly had all the excuses to feel sorry for myself, but I decided to just keep trying until I got life right!

My mother worked at many jobs and was finally hired by an incentive travel company. She married again to a widower with six children. It was a merger of lots of personalities, talents, and ideas. It allowed all of us to have a somewhat stable life. They added one more boy to the family to make it an even ten kids, seven boys and three girls.

We had a big dinner table, and the logistics of shopping, preparing, and scheduling meals would make your head spin. Each child had their own set of chores and activities: soccer, basketball, baseball, football practices, and games to attend. It was a three-mile walk to the Jr. High from our home. So, our Stepfather would pick us up after school. His law practice work didn't end at 3:40 like our school, and he had twelve mouths to feed. We would wait in the bushes in front of the school until he could come get us, which was occasionally as late as 7 or 8 PM. Dinner was sometimes waiting on the table for us and sometimes staying warm in the oven.

We were all quite active in High School. My mother must have been exhausted all of the time, but we had a great role model for how to succeed and rise to the challenges in life through her! One of my new brothers was extremely smart and would be labeled as Obsessive/Compulsive these days. I was amazed at the way he organized his things for school, for sports, and around himself at home. We shared a bulletin board, and the push pins on his side were always in a perfectly straight line… even the extra pins. His handwriting was also perfect, with perfect circles to dot the "i's."

We were both on the swim team in high school. He and I would make the 6 AM swim workout before school and 3 to 6 PM workout after school. After that was dinner, chores, then homework.

We were both socially active but disciplined in our focus. We were all expected to make good grades!

One of my greatest High School achievements happened in my senior year. The Spring Pep Rally was held in the auditorium. All the Spring sports participants were recognized, and achievements were awarded. There was baseball, tennis, track and field, and finally, swimming.

We had a good swim relay team, of which I was a member. So I went up on stage when they called my name "Mac Churchill, our All-State Breaststroker."

The auditorium broke out in laughter, sparse applause, snickers, and some stunned silence. It's a name association that trumps all the big stud football players. My classmates are still talking about my achievements. I remind them that with dedicated practice, they too can master the Smooth Stroke.

I am occasionally asked to demonstrate my technique, but I must remind them (to quote a famous song) that "I am not as good as I once was but I am good once as I ever was."

To this day, the story is always good for some laughs!

Chapter 10

California Check In

At one point, while waiting for my Bone Marrow transplant, I was getting a transfusion every ten days. We were in California visiting grandkids, and I needed a transfusion. Since it was a Saturday, the large hospital system that my doctor normally would have used was not open. He directed us to a small hospital thirty minutes away. I was very lethargic and needed a transfusion to be able to fly back to Ft Worth.

We were instructed to be at the hospital at 8 AM. We arrived on time.

The receptionist/check-in administrative assistant told us to have a seat.

"I have never checked someone into the hospital before; the regular person is sick today," she told us.

Well, you can imagine how this was going to play out. I answered her as she slowly came to each question. She was hunting for the keys and typing with one finger extremely slowly. When she got bogged down, she would call in the IT guy to come over from another building to help with the computer. She called for his assistance two more times.

Will this ever end?

Finally, about 11:30 AM, three and a half hours after we'd arrived, we were finished.

"Hold on. You are over 65, aren't you?" she asked. "Yes, ma'am."

My lips were a thin white line by this time. "The State of California requires me to ask you these 20 additional questions."

She started out asking some of the same questions that had already been asked. Then she asked, "Have you ever used an alias?" She had never looked up the entire time she had been trying to get me signed in.

"Why, YES, ma'am, I have."

"And what is that?"

"George Clooney," Her head shot straight up, as well as the other people in the waiting room. All eyes were on me.

The resemblance was not even close, and everyone smiled and sighed in disappointment.

After four hours of checking in, we were finally registered. I considered this a world record for the length of time to check in!

We were then led into a procedure room with a bed to lie down on, a warm blanket, and pillows under my elbows. Next was a blood draw to confirm my blood type. I started out deathly afraid of needles, but you get used to it over time. This became the needle stick from heck!

The first try was from the nurse's assistant. She tried valiantly. Three determined pokes, and it was time to call the head nurse. The nurse apologized for the previous efforts but assured me that the head nurse would be successful. There was so very little blood in my veins that the blood vessels had shriveled. I was a hard target, but she was determined. She tried to get the vein three times and then called the emergency room nurse, who brought a hand-held ultrasound device that showed the location of the vessels.

He was successful on the second poke.

They started the IV. Who would've thought that the hardest part of the process would have been registration and the IV insertion!? The silver lining was that it did allow me to lie in bed and watch a Texas Longhorn football game.

And they won!! I went to the University of Texas and have been a lifelong fan so that put a smile on my face!

I do want to thank the team that helped me get my transfusion.

I would not have been able to get back home without their help. They each gave up a Saturday to do my procedure. Leaving the hospital, The Eagles' song, "Hotel California," began playing in my mind.

One thing I have learned in this fight with cancer is that no matter how bad you have it, someone has it worse. Putting a smile on someone's face may be the most important thing to happen to them that day.

Chapter 11
Jeremiah Was A Bullfrog

My wife has been with me all the way in this fight against cancer.

She has attended every doctor's visit with me. She had to drive me to Dallas from Ft. Worth for every appointment. She has quite literally saved my life on multiple occasions. This has been tough for both of us, but we have grown so much closer. We feel like we know what is really important in life and really enjoy life more than ever.

This journey in the cancer fight has introduced me to many Earthly Angels. One such Angel nursed me along during my recovery from the Bone Marrow Transplant. Joyce brought sunshine to my quarantine existence. She shaved my head, made sure I was bathed, ate properly, and made sure I took my medication. There were twenty-three different prescriptions!

A few weeks into my 30-day hospital recovery stay, we developed a happy routine. When she walked into my room at 7 AM to start her shift, I started with a song I customized for Joyce.

Jeremiah was a bullfrog Was a good friend of mine

I never understood a single word he said But I helped him drink his wine

And he always had some mighty fine wine Singing Joyce to the world

All the boys and girls now

Joyce to the fishes in the deep blue sea Joyce to you and me

Joyce would do a little happy shuffle dance while I sang. Wow! That was exactly the way to start the day off! I smile every time that song is on the radio or television and thank God for Joyce.

Humor can be a powerful tool for coping with difficult emotions.

Chapter 12

Lunch With Ben Hogan

Hospital bound, I often found myself reminiscing, and one of my favorite memories is of my lunches with the famous golfer Ben Hogan.

I had the privilege of working with Mr. Hogan on his Cadillac purchases. I was an officer in the Frank Kent Cadillac dealership in Fort Worth, Texas. When Mr. Hogan needed a new car or service, he would get in touch with Mr. Kent, who then contacted me. I would do the legwork, and I was able to develop a friendly relationship with Mr. Hogan.

We were both members of Shady Oaks Country Club. The club was close to the Cadillac dealership, so I would occasionally go to the club for lunch. When I would arrive at the dining room, Mr. Hogan was usually seated at the Round Table in the corner of the room. He would motion to me to sit next to him on his right-hand side. Our chairs looked out over the 18th green and number ten tee box.

One occasion found us discussing something quite mundane when a golfer came up on his golf cart. The golfer proceeded into the dining room where we were sitting. The golfer approached one of the waiters, Charles, and asked if he could visit with Mr. Hogan.

Charles took him over to Mr. Hogan. The golfer said, "I bet you don't remember me, Mr. Hogan, but last year at this time, I hit a ball and it over shot the green. The ball hit that window in front of you. You came outside and picked it up, and handed it back to me. You told me that if I had Hogan balls and Hogan clubs, this wouldn't have happened.

Well, Mr. Hogan, I bought Hogan balls and Hogan clubs, and in this tournament today, I just had a hole-in-one. Would you mind signing my ball for me?"

"No, I sure don't. In fact, bring me all your balls, and I'll sign 'em all."

So, the player went back out to his cart and brought back five or six balls. Mr. Hogan gladly signed all the balls and made that hole-in-one a memory like no other for the golfer. What a souvenir that was!

Mr. Hogan didn't autograph many balls.

Another occasion found us talking about nothing in particular when something made Mr. Hogan remember his start on the pro tour.

"Mac, have I told you about my start on the tour?" he asked.

"No, sir."

"Well, I was headed to California, and I hitched a ride with another pro who was headed out there. We drove, and when we got there, five of us shared the accommodations. They all went out to dinner, and I stayed back to wash my soxx out in the sink. Then I went outside and picked three or four oranges off the tree for dinner."

I think Mr. Hogan would be surprised at how things have changed and how popular golf is now!

On another occasion, we were respectfully interrupted by Charles, the head waiter. Charles whispered something into Mr. Hogan's ear.

"Well, Mac, you'll have to excuse me; they are ready for me upstairs."

"The Japanese are upstairs and are ready for pictures. They built a golf hole in Guam that I 'designed.' They named the hole after me. They have flown into town, and they are ready for pictures. So, I had better go upstairs." I tell this story just to show how respectful and what a gentleman he was, even though there was a 37-year age difference between us.

On another day, when we were having lunch at The Round Table. Mr. Hogan was talking, and something reminded him of his days as a young man caddying at Glen Gardens Country Club. Mr. Hogan said that he carried a golf bag 18 holes for a doctor on this particular day. When they finished the round, the doctor gave him a left-handed mashie for a tip.

Mr. Hogan said that when the day was finished, all the caddies would go to the driving range. They would all hit balls. Whoever hit the ball the shortest distance would be required to go pick up all the balls. This was before the golf cart with the rake behind it that would pick up the balls. He said that he had to pick up a lot of balls while learning to hit that left-handed mashie. He was right-handed.

I tell this story to express the determination Mr. Hogan exhibited throughout his life. Even after he retired, I remember Mr. Hogan practicing. Hitting bags of balls daily to a shag boy named Martin Thompson. Martin would have a towel wrapped around his hand and would be stationed at the opposite end of the practice area. When Mr. Hogan would hit an iron shot, Martin would catch it in the towel wrapped around his hand. Then Martin would simply let the ball drop into the Shag bag at his feet. Martin might have to reach or stretch if Mr. Hogan was hitting a fairway wood. I can only imagine that if I was hitting a fairway wood, poor Martin would need a motorcycle to even have a chance of catching the ball.

I don't think anyone could outwork Mr. Hogan. Even after he retired, Mr. Hogan worked on his game, hitting shag bags full of balls.

Mr. Hogan was a very loyal person. If you were his friend, you really had a friend. Since I sold him his Cadillacs, he expected loyalty in return. The golf pro at Shady Oaks said Mr. Hogan would check my golf bag to make sure that I was playing Hogan clubs. To this day, I carry a couple of Hogan clubs out of respect for a man I loved and admired. He was another example of the determination it takes to succeed in whatever life throws your way.

Chapter 13

Anti War

While recovering in the hospital, you get plenty of time to remember events in your past. Some smells, faces, or words can fish them out of the dusty storage bins of our minds. One that I recalled was a trip across the UT campus when I was a student. This was a time when the Vietnam War turmoil swept across our nation and our campus.

I was leaving the Business School for lunch at the fraternity house. I didn't have to be at the fraternity house immediately, so I thought I would see what and why some students (and probably outside agitators) were saying about this war that was halfway around the world in a country most of us had never heard of. There were lots of opinions about the US involvement; some were for it, and some were against it. I heard this group of students discussing the upcoming Peace March. I wanted to hear the differing opinion, so I stopped to listen.

We were all standing in a loose circle on the Main Plaza. The current speaker was dressed in the new anti-war 60's "hippie" style, complete with long and greasy hair, a droopy long mustache, a vintage army fatigue jacket, and bell-bottom jeans, which were becoming popular with a group of people who apparently didn't like to bathe.

"We need to burn some flags if we really want to get their attention." "We need to shoot some pigs; that'll show 'em."

"We need to slash some tires. We need to burn some cars to show the pigs who is in control!"

"Pig" was the derogatory word for police.

Inflammatory speech was used around the circle for a few minutes, with each making their opinion known.

Well, naturally, I had to jump in when there was a pause.

"Are you talking about a Peace March around campus?" I asked. "If you are, the actions you are discussing would be more like a riot and not a Peace March. The TV coverage would emphasize the NON-Peaceful nature of the March. It just seems to me you would be defeating the purpose of a Peace March. Gandhi clearly demonstrated the success of nonviolent resistance."

There were clearly elements in these groups who were not there for a Peace March. They seemed older, not students and their focus was a violent overthrow of our government.

Then, our group joined eight to ten other groups on the plaza and headed into the UT board room. I had never seen a board room this large. The University Of Texas Board Room held what seemed like 80 students. All of them were talking at the same time. Slowly, the crowd allowed some to speak freely without interrupting. Then, one person stood in the middle of the room and pointed at me and said, "This guy thinks we should be more peaceful. Let's hear what he has to say."

I stepped forward, took a deep breath, and began to feel really uncomfortable and out of place! Yikes! I was only 19 years old, and I was advocating restraint. A Peace March should be peaceful. Seemed simple enough to me. I explained my reasoning to an animated crowd of organizers.

Amazingly, they let me speak without interruption.

When I finished, I stepped back and tried to disappear into the crowd. Looking around the room. I decided that I really didn't fit into this crowd. There was no one here that I recognized. They were just curious students who were bored with classes and were looking for a little excitement. So, I began to slowly back up and work my way out of the room. It was time for me to get away from here!

After the Peace March, the news reported thousands marching and a few slashed tires, but overall, it was a relatively Peaceful March.

Later that semester, the Anti-War demonstrations and open discussions on campus were happening every day. All institutions across the country were under attack: schools, government, and businesses.

We had weekly fraternity chapter meetings. The anti-war sentiment had begun to divide our fraternity into those who strongly opposed the war and those in favor of the Vietnam War.

That night, there was another protest on campus. This created a huge split in the fraternity.

Those supporting the anti-war effort went to join the protests on campus. Those opposed were attending the fraternity chapter meeting. I felt that this was ripping the fraternity chapter apart. I was the President of our fraternity chapter. I had to lead the meeting. Half of the chapter was on campus with very strong feelings, and the other half was at our meeting with equally strong feelings. Those who were at the meeting were condemning those who were on campus. A definite split was forming. What could I do? This had the markings of disaster for our fraternity.

The call to order was made in the chapter meeting. Still, some were mumbling about the missing members on campus.

"Brothers, a lot of our members are on campus tonight joining the war protest (more mumbling). But where are all the girls?"

Everyone began looking around and at each other.

"They are on campus!! We can have a chapter meeting any night. Why don't we adjourn and see what's happening on campus?"

Yeah, let's do it! Great idea," they all cheered.

We all adjourned to join the protests on campus, just for different reasons. So, girls saved our chapter, and life went on. This lesson in crisis management served me well later in life.

"Making lemonade out of lemons" opportunities will arise throughout your life. Let the opportunities to turn a disagreeable job into a successful one put a smile on your face when you recognize them.

Chapter 14
Support Groups

Thursday luncheon group

A group of 10 of us gather each Thursday for lunch. We started doing this as different ones of us began to slow our work schedules and/or retire. We picked a different restaurant to visit each week. This restaurant hopping allows us to try out new restaurants when they open. We have become the unofficial reviewers for what is new in town. Even our kids look to us to tell them, "How it was."

This weekly get-together allows us to check in with each other. We catch up on each other's experiences, our families, and our latest travels. We discuss all the sports topics: football, basketball, golf, and other hot news topics.

Friday lunch buddies

A buddy from elementary school and I get together each Saturday for lunch. He lost his wife over a year ago. He had retired, and he and his wife had moved back to Fort Worth from South Carolina. They left many friends back in South Carolina. They renewed many friendships. This offers us both a chance to discuss sports and whatever is newsworthy that week. We recently added another Combatant to our luncheon. He is fighting an unknown medical condition. They are still running tests on him to identify the cause of his problem. Now, there are more of us to help carry the other guy's load.

Prayer groups

Friends have entered my name on several prayer lists. I don't think you can be on too many lists. I know that there have been many moments that can't be explained by anything other than answered prayers.

Survivor friends

I have mutually bonded with other survivors of cancer. We may have all suffered different types of cancer, but whatever type it is, it still requires a fight for life. All of us have stories that make the journey of fighting cancer not quite as lonely. We all have advice for each other- Some of these are:

1) Work out whenever you can, even if it is in bed or taking short walks.
2) Watch your nutrition. It's important that your body receives the proper nutrition to fight your cancer. I was introduced to a nutritional drink while recovering from my bone marrow transplant. Most of the food and energy drinks tasted metallic and distasteful.

Kate Farms. Originally recommended by the nutritionist after my Bone Marrow Transplant. This is a meal replacement shake that is plant-based and made from organic ingredients. Kate Farms does not typically contain caffeine, which is so prevalent in other name-brand energy drinks. So many times, chemotherapy will make food taste bad, and this will help your body have the necessary nutrition to get you through those times.

Every day, I start with a small carton of Kate Farms Chocolate over ice. Starts my day off right with good nutrients.

3) Stay hydrated. Your body will reach a certain point of balance and throw off unnecessary water. Water will flush out the bad elements in your body as well as help keep your veins flowing.

4) Wear rubber-soled shoes for traction

5) Drink little if any alcohol. You never know how the alcohol chemicals will react with your medicine.

6) Keep praying, and don't give up. The rapidity at which they are making medical advances is amazing! Just hang in there long enough for researchers to find a cure.

7) Keep a positive spirit, and don't be afraid to make someone smile.

8) Walking a dog will give you a reason to exercise daily. This forced exercise will go a long way to keeping you healthy. This will be influenced by where you are in your cycle of care.

9) Men should wear black underwear.

10) Different medications and our reactions to them can cause unpleasant accidents. We never know when it might happen.

11) Shower or bathe with a light, fresh-scented body wash. All of the chemicals that are being injected, infused, or transfused into your body will exit through your pores and as well as normal routes. Those smells can be really strong, especially when they are mixed with our anxieties! Avoid wearing perfumes, hair products, and even deodorants that are scented. All of our senses are under attack by chemicals, and each patient might react differently than others to something that might normally be pleasant.

Workout buddies

Three days a week, I join my workout buddies at the gym. We all talk about everything normal. It is so comforting and reassuring to be "Normal."

We can just talk about sports or our latest trips while keeping our body parts moving. This is a proven way to keep yourself healthy, both mentally and physically.

Breakfast Group

Out breakfast group of 50 men has been meeting for over 50 years. There are some members who are younger, and they bring in new ideas and experiences. We are made up of different disciplines: bankers, lawyers, doctors, pilots, insurance, auto sales, etc. It's a great place to check in and let everyone know that you are still alive. We have a great breakfast to start the day. It is also a great forum for the exchange of ideas and keeps the brain active. Through the input of our members and occasional guest speakers, we are all able to stay current on politics and business happening around us.

Family

How would anyone make it without family support? I am sure that it can be done, but it must be extremely difficult. We have a blended family of children from our previous marriages. She treats my children with the same love as her own. Her philosophy, and now mine, is, "Children and Grandchildren can never be loved too much."

My family has supported us in big ways and small, big in terms of ambulance runs, long waits at the hospital, and lots of prayers that are so comforting. They are always ready to help take some of the burdens off of us. My "Trophy Wife" has been my constant companion throughout this fight. She has driven me to every appointment. She has sat in on every doctor's review and treatment. She has listened to the doctor explain the treatment and recovery process. She knows that she might need to "re-explain" or repeat something when we get home. Most of the time, she answers all the medication questions they ask of me. She applied all her nursing skills for my post-treatment recovery, although she didn't study nursing in school. She researches everything online and asks the doctors and nurses lots of questions. She learned the skill of applying and removing bandages and how to move or lift a weak and recovering husband.

She makes sure that I take the correct medicine at the correct time. She alerts the doctors about any suspect conditions that may have arisen since our last visit. Many of the doctor visits found me too weak to think or focus.

Men who would not go to a doctor until an arm fell off become quite dependent and "Baby Like." Men rely on their caretakers like never before. We have always been the strong ones, with less emotional display and less dependence. Suddenly, we are brought to our knees. Our world is turned upside down. We are dependent and weaker in many ways. Some men lash out in anger, some withdraw, and some fight with all their strength.

My fight with cancer never became easy, just less difficult with humor. Humor seems to reduce stress for all involved in the fight. When Ronald Reagan, after he had been shot in an attempted assassination was being wheeled into the operating room for surgery, he looked up at the doctors and said, "I hope you are all Republicans."

Try to put a smile on someone's face every day. You'll both feel better.

Chapter 15
Catheter Extraction

Before my neck cancer surgery, I had to have a catheter installed. This was not a personal request (trust me) but necessary for the surgery. The nurse arrived to install something the size of an elephant trunk (don't trust me on this one). Initially flattered, I had to ask, "You are going to do what with that?" Her reply was a little smirk and I immediately knew she was in control. Well, the neck surgery took twelve hours and involved four doctors.

Actually, all I know is that I woke up with this thing attached to me. After a few days of recovery, it was time to remove my new Best Friend. Believe me, I have never treated any of my friends with the respect I treated this fellow.

The nurse arrived. It was time to go to work. My "friend" had to leave. We were close, but a little too close. Parting wasn't really sad. I closed my eyes. I couldn't bear to watch him leave.

Everything worked out fine. Very professional. No pain. That's what really happened.

But that was not what I told everyone who came into my room after she picked up her tools and went to her next victim or patient. My description of the procedure was as wild as a Hollywood thriller!

Everyone expects the worst. So, I made up a very entertaining story.

She came in dressed in a black Hazmat Suit, looking around to make sure there were no witnesses. She leaned over and made the sign of the cross over me and mumbled something. She reached into her bag and pulled out a large pair of pliers. She lifted up my gown and suppressed a controlled giggle. She then asked me to grab my private and lean back. She then pulled a chair up to the end of the bed, sat down, and braced her feet against the end of the bed. She bent over with her pliers in hand. She grabbed the exposed end of the catheter with the pliers and yanked!

Yeoweeee! That hurt! Then she offered it to me in case I or a friend, needed it for an operation in the future or if I wanted to keep it as a souvenir.

No one believed my tale, but we all had a good laugh. We escaped the stress of the day, if only for a moment. My wife won't let me tell the grandsons this story!

Chapter 16

Lemons

Lemonade out of lemons

We cannot live life without facing adversity. How we deal with this adversity will determine the direction of our life. A positive spirit can aid greatly in overcoming adversity. A positive spirit will look at a problem and ask, "How can I turn this situation into a positive one? In other words, how can I make lemonade out of lemons?

How can I best use my recovery time? Call long-time customers and thank them for their loyal support of your company. Maybe fix or repair something around the house that you have been putting off. Depending upon your condition, you could volunteer for a charity religious organization, expand a hobby, or focus more on family time. The choices are endless.

A positive-spirited person will look for ways to be useful. Rather than sitting around wringing their hands, they will look for things to accomplish and not get depressed. It can be as little as feeding themselves or taking on a civic project — all reflective of their condition.

Chapter 17
Johnny Depp

I had just completed a 12-hour and four doctor surgery on my head and neck. They had removed a fast-growing tumor surrounding my carotid artery. The doctors removed part of my jaw, 2/3 of my ear and ear canal, and adjacent affected tissues.

During my recovery, the Johnny Depp trial was going on. Now, there was a guy in worse shape than me. Johnny had to be going through more pain than I could imagine. Adding to his pain was his inability to work.

Working with my doctors, we discussed the reconstruction of my ear. Poor Johnny looked like he was going to be tied up with this trial for quite a while, and I needed to be ready to fill in as Jack Sparrow in his upcoming movies. We couldn't limit my options to just Jack Sparrow, either. I might be needed as a "stand-in" for other stars who find themselves in awkward situations.

The doctor needed to create a "Variety Pack" so I could be ready at a moment's notice. The Pack to replace my ear would contain:

1) A Jack Sparrow ear
2) A Shrek Ear
3) A Dr. Spock ear

4) A Bugs Bunny ear (Dr's recommendation)
5) A George Clooney ear (to match the rest of my body)

Replacing Johnny Depp while he was up to his eyeballs in his lawsuit would surely earn me an Academy Award!

We then began to plan with the nurses who would join me in the limousine for the Academy Awards show. What kind of champagne would we drink? Finally, how many tickets would we need for the Academy Awards show? Who would join me on the Red Carpet? Our imaginations went wild with how much fun we would have. Then, we began a list of people to thank.

The limo driver that brought us to the show The usher that showed us to our seats

My favorite nurses and their significant others

My fourth-grade teacher, Mrs. Barse who, taught me how to hold a pencil

My fifth-grade teacher, Mrs. Loving, that taught me how to draw. My high school swimming teammates Andy, Ted, and Mark.

My high school history teacher, Mr. Cozine, taught me that it was hard to kill Rasputin, the mad monk.

Mr. Ford, my Boy Scout troop leader, taught me how to make a fire

Ms. Abbott, my dog trainer, for freeing me up to attend tonight's presentation.

An hour later, I would wind it up thanking the Academy for their wise choice.

Finally, my trophy wife for her encouragement to give up a comedy career and concentrate on more dramatic roles. I think she will appreciate this romantic touch at the end.

My wife just sat in the exam room shaking her head.

This was all done in great fun… Relieving stress and laughing.

Chapter 18

Gentleman's Club

F ive weeks after my transplant surgery, I was home recovering. While taking a morning shower, I completely stopped all motion. I don't remember any of that, but that is how my wife described it. She said she found me motionless in the shower. She turned the shower off and got a chair to sit me in. She then called my brother to help her muscle me out of the shower.

After a quick call for an ambulance, I was transported to the hospital in Dallas. We arrived at the emergency room to be examined, and a series of tests were performed over several hours. I don't remember any of this. I was later assigned to an observation room. That is a room with a glass wall so that doctors and staff can observe the patient without coming into the room.

I was hooked up to electronic monitors. They shaved my head and attached leads to monitor for brain waves. Late one night, I called my wife and told her to pick me up on the curb downstairs. I was ready to go home, although I didn't know where I was or why! She reacted quickly and notified the nurses' station.

They said that they would stop the "break out." They had it under control, and there would be no escape. For almost five days,

I did not respond to nurses' or doctors' questions. I received food and medicine from an IV.

Five days of tests and observation went by before the fog began to clear, and I had begun to comply with simple instructions from the nurses.

UT Southwestern is a teaching hospital, so visits by interns, residents, doctors, and nurses are routine. I had just finished an early breakfast when a group of about eight people came into my room. Leading the Neurology department parade was a doctor, followed by residents, interns, three nurses, and the head pharmacist.

"Welcome back, Mr. Churchill. How are you feeling?" asked the teaching doctor.

"Good to be back in the game."

"I would like to ask you some questions to test your cognitive ability."

"OK, shoot."

"Do you know where you are?"

"Yes, sir, I am at UT Southwestern Hospital."

"Do you know which city we are in?"

"Yes, sir, we are in Dallas."

"Do you know who the President is?"

"Yes, sir, it is Donald Trump."

Then he reached up for one of his ID and access badges hanging from one of the many lanyards around his neck. He held one out for me to see.

"Mr. Churchill, Do you know what this is?"

"Sure, I said. That is your Lifetime Membership Badge to the Gentlemen's Club!"

The room went quiet. No one knew how to react. What if it was true?

But then, the doctor began laughing.

Everyone took a deep breath, and we all laughed! I think the doctor knew I was back. I bet when the story was retold, it got some good laughs.

Chapter 19

Leeches

Blood cancer can require blood transfusions on a regular basis. I was diagnosed with Myelodysplastic Syndrome. This is a cancer that destroys red blood cells that carry oxygen and nutrients throughout the body. The therapy was to have transfusions every ten days before my Bone Marrow Transplant.

Some of the time, I would need one pint of blood, but most of the time, I would need two pints of blood. The process takes about 1–3 hours per unit of blood, but it is not painful. I had transfusions for almost a year before having a Bone Marrow transplant.

The side effect of receiving healthy donated blood is a build-up of iron in the liver. This build-up can cause liver damage. So, the solution is a phlebotomy to reduce the amount of iron in one's body.

The technicians start an IV that will drain a specific amount of blood.

The blood that is drained takes the extra iron with it.

After several of these procedures, the iron levels return to normal. So, after I checked in at the receptionist desk, the tech or nurse would walk us back to the procedure room. The conversation would start off something like this as we are being led through the maze of halls. "So, do you have my leeches picked out?" I asked.

"We sure do!"

"Well, last time, they were underfed, and they were ravenous!"

"We have picked out the best leeches in the colony just for you!"

None of this conversation made me more comfortable about what was about to happen to me. We arrived in the procedure room, and they began to ask the routine medical questions. When the nurse said she was going to take my temperature, I cautiously asked if she was "going to take my temperature like the nurse did last time I was here?"

"What way was that?"

"Well, she made me drop my pants and promptly swiped my butt with the thermometer!"

Laughing, she insisted, "No, she did not!"

"Well, maybe I have that confused with another one of the admission procedures. Are those leeches ready? I would like to pick out my own leeches."

You can never be too cautious when selecting the right leach.

I was seated in a reclining chair with pillows under my elbows and a warm blanket over me. The blood pressure monitor was purring.

"You know, it just occurred to me that since we are going to be here a while, you might want to hear me yodel," I said.

They have long ago figured out that I'm just joking with them, and this is to make the time pass quicker.

"Probably not, but Alphonse here sings in the Dallas Opera." Alphonse is one of the nurses in the room.

"Is this true, Alphonse? You really can sing opera?"

"Yes, I do and have for a number of years. Do you want to hear an aria?"

"By all means! Let's hear something from 'La Traviata'."

"I will after I hear you yodel," he called my bluff.

"Dang man, you called my bluff; I can't yodel, but I can clog. Go ahead and show us your stuff!"

Alphonse sang a beautiful aria. His voice carried down the hall to the other nearby exam rooms. The performance was brief but so special!

We were amazed at his hidden talent and privileged to hear him share his passion.

A side note to this beautiful experience. My Trophy Wife and I were invited to the Ft Worth Opera many years before I became ill. We were guests of the President of the Opera Association and his wife. We had a lovely dinner and wine before the performance, then walked across the street and sat in the President's box.

The box provided a great view of the stage. The lights went down as the orchestra began tuning their instruments, and so did I. My wife said she spent the night elbowing me, trying to wake me up or at least stop my snoring. It had been a long day, and I was just conditioned to go to sleep when it got that dark!

We were never invited back. Guess I'll have to learn to snore in Italian!

Chapter 20

George Clooney Close the Drapes

With each examination and each procedure and radiation treatment, I was asked to remove my shirt. I said, "Sure, I will if you will draw the curtains and close the door."

Puzzled looks would ensue, but the nurses were accustomed to a patient's desire for modesty and would always comply with their wishes. I felt like I should explain my personal need for modesty to them.

"It's just that every time I take my shirt off, the nurses come rushing into the room if they happen to be passing by. They think I look like George Clooney. I would like to avoid the confusion and disappointment when they realize their mistake."

Naturally, this brings a momentary chuckle and a smile. Some would join in the fun and say they did see a resemblance and would try to protect my identity! They probably don't see the same physique in the exam room that I see in my mirror at home.

I have had a lot of fun with them over the years. They most always smile, knowing they probably were not about to be stampeded by all of the nurses on the floor.

Chapter 21
Hondo Crouch

W hile recovering in the hospital, I remembered meeting a man who would become a Texas legend. I had been invited to join a group of football players in Fredericksburg, Texas. I had become friends with these players since many of them attended our fraternity parties. The football players were members of the 1969 University of Texas National Championship team. Those guys were like Greek Gods on campus at that time. A road trip with them was better than going to Disneyland.

There were about 12 of us headed to Fredericksburg's 125th Anniversary Celebration. Fredericksburg is a beautiful small town set in the Texas Hill Country. It is known for its German heritage and beer halls. We immediately began sampling some of their best beers to start the celebration.

Time passed quickly. Then, it was time for Governor Preston Smith to speak on the town square. Our group was invited to go listen to the speech. Remember, our group was treated like Greek Gods. The Governor wanted to have Texas Best in his audience. The only problem was that a few in the group were beyond a few beers and began to make unsolicited comments.

The Texas Rangers (lawmen) recognized that the situation could become embarrassing for all concerned, especially the Governor. They gathered us like sheep and led us to a beer stand across the courthouse lawn. While leaning against the beer stand, I bumped into a true Texas Character— Hondo Crouch.

Hondo and I just seemed to click. He wore a red bandana neatly tied around his neck, cowboy jeans, a Western belt, a denim shirt, boots, and silver hair tucked neatly under his rugged and worn cowboy hat. Hondo was the real deal. He must have thought I was a member of the Championship team. I let him know that I wasn't but felt like a dog handler with 11 Dobermans on a leash. Hondo was a swimmer at UT, and I had been a swimmer in high school. A couple of beers later, he said,

"Mac, I bought a town today!"

"You did! Where is this town?"

"It's close by. Just up the road."

"What's the name of the town you bought?"

"Lukenbach, Texas"

"Looking back where?"

"No, No, Lukenbach!"

"Yeah, but looking back, where?"

"No, let me try again. Lukenbach is the name of the town."

"Why did you buy it?"

"I just wanted a place where me and my friends could get away to."

I didn't have any idea that his list of friends included Waylon Jennings, Willie Nelson, and the boys.

"Hondo, congratulations on the purchase of your town. I will have to come visit you sometime."

He was a gentleman rancher and a fine person and was a pleasure to be around, even if it was only one afternoon.

Of course, 7-8 years later, the song came out, and I learned how to pronounce Lukenbach, Texas. When the song would play on the radio, it would take me back to that idyllic afternoon in Fredericksburg.

Chapter 22

Emergency Room Porn

I was undressing and getting ready to go to bed one night when my wife noticed that the left side of my face had drooped. She asked if I could blink my left eye. I couldn't move anything on that side. She asked me to lift my left arm. I could move my arm, but it felt heavy. We had both seen an email about how to recognize a stroke. I didn't feel any pain in my chest, but she thought we should go to the emergency room just to be sure.

I had a large (3" X 4") squamous cell cancer taken off the top of my head in January of that year. By March, I was having shooting pain in my left ear, but nothing showed up on any of the CT, PET scans, or Ultrasound tests.

We left home for UT Southwestern in Dallas since they had all of my medical records. Upon arrival, they pulled up my medical history. The ER Doctor on duty asked me to open and close my eyes. The left side of my face didn't move. Then she asked me to raise my left arm, and I could raise it, but it took a lot of effort. She thought I had Bell's Palsy instead of a stroke, which was better since it would go away in a few weeks, and a stroke could cause permanent damage. She would call a neurologist for verification.

It was a Sunday evening. We arrived at the hospital at 8:45 PM. The emergency room was packed, and the wait began. We watched the home improvement channel for 6 hours. I learned to tell subway tile from floor tile! We finally got into an exam room around 3 AM. We were exhausted.

The doctor arrived and performed some tests. He confirmed that I was not having a stroke but that it was Bell's Palsy. He apologized for the long wait, but they were swamped with all kinds of emergencies. He said he would send in his nurse to finalize the paperwork for release and get me a prescription to slow the symptoms.

The nurse showed up and began reviewing all of the routine details. We were tired and wanted to go home.

After a battery of questions, she asked, "Do you have any questions?"

"Why yes, I do. The doctor couldn't help me, but he assured me that you could. Do you know what channel the Porn is on?"

She looked at her clipboard and processed my question. My wife broke out laughing! The nurse spun around and headed for me with a smile on her face. She was exhausted, too, and knew how tired and stressed out we must have been.

She put one hand on my arm, took one of my hands in her other hand, and said, "Thanks for making me laugh. I needed that. It's been a long, tense day."

We both joined my wife in stress-relieving laughter. Laughter is even healthy at 4 AM.

We finally got home around 5 AM and literally fell into bed. Our nurse would still be on duty for a few more hours. God bless her. We often forget the stress and pressure that our caregivers must endure while they care for us. A smile seems to relieve them, if only for a short time. I have overheard them retelling the story to relieve another person's stress.

Mac Churchill

I am so glad that I could put a smile on someone's face and make their day a little better.

Chapter 23
The Professional Salesman

The conventional image of a salesman is that of fast-talking, greasy hair, and wearing a leisure suit. The exact opposite is true of a successful salesman. If a salesman doesn't listen to the customer and identify the customer's needs, he will have little chance of selling anything.

Why is selling so hard? Well, I think it comes from a lack of the right kind of sales training. That is, the sales training concentration is focused on product knowledge. How does this feature of your product do this or that? Frankly, your customer doesn't care how knowledgeable you are if it will not solve their problem. How do you find out what problem the customer needs to solve? You simply slow down and ask.

Slow down and ask. Now you may ask, what kind of sales advice is that? Let me relate a true story of how this was implemented many years ago. A long time ago, before computers, typewriters were the machines that increased productivity. Each year, companies improve their products. The companies just knew that their new typewriter was so great that if it was shown to customers with old-style machines, they would buy it. So, off the salesmen went to the office buildings. Trailing behind them was the latest typewriter on a dolly. There were one or two salesmen on each floor in the office building, and 2 or 3 more salesmen were on the elevators, all with typewriters in tow.

Each year, IBM held a National Awards recognition dinner. Every year, the same individual won the National Sales Award. Each year, they cut his territory in half. The executives were amazed at this performance. Was he just Lucky? What special technique did he have? He didn't seem to work any harder. There were other salesmen who knew far more about typewriters than he did. How could he possibly outsell every other salesman year after year?

The executives set him down after the presentation and asked him how he did it. He said, "It is really quite simple. You know those other salesmen are towing around our latest typewriters? Well. I don't take a typewriter with me."

"Well, how could you possibly sell anyone a typewriter without showing it to them?"

"I simply ask the secretary two questions. What do you like most about the typewriter you are using now?"

They will usually talk about how easy the touch, automatic carriage return, or other features are to use. This allows me to ask the second question. "What features do you like least about your typewriter?"

They may say a number of features. So, guess what kind of typewriter I show up with the next day? It's really quite easy and time-efficient.

You can quickly see that the same principle would work in real estate, cars, airplanes, computers, or financial services. I will have a product with all of the desired features and none of the unnecessary or objectionable features.

I have used the two questions for years. One occasion I remember was when an older couple pulled up to the Cadillac dealership in an almost new Volvo.

Well, on the surface, this looked like a tough nut. You could tell that he was a successful businessman who was retired, and his wife was driving him. So, I began my two-question inquiry. They mentioned safety and the turning radius. I then asked what they liked least. He blew up, "That blankety, blank car doesn't have power in the right front seat, and that's where I sit!"

It really became quite easy because we showed him the car with all of the features he wanted.

Another occasion found me taking a call from one of our longtime customers. "Mac, I would like to get a new car," she said. After some discussion, I told her I would be right out to her home.

Upon arrival, she welcomed me in and showed me the car she would be trading in. I took down the pertinent numbers and noted that her car was two years old, with only 300 miles. When we went back inside, I asked my two questions. She said she liked the car just fine. She didn't drive much anymore. She usually had someone take her to the beauty shop or wherever she wanted to go. Further, she added that she had given a good sum of money to the Boys Club.

"Mac, I just like the feeling of independence knowing that my car is sitting there if I ever need it." She said every morning, she got up and drank her coffee, then she would go to the sink to wash out her cup and look out the window over the sink. "There sits my yellow Seville, and I'm tired of the color."

"Well, ma'am, what color would you like?"

You know, if you think about it, we are all salesmen. Use the two questions to make more sales and save yourself time.

So many salespeople are filled with product knowledge that when they get in front of a prospect, they explode with information.

I call this "hunting with a shotgun." They seem to fill the sky with shots (information), hoping something falls out of the sky. This becomes a hit-or- miss proposition. This method is used every day by young, enthusiastic, and nervous salespeople. This method can work, but it requires a lot more prospects and much more work.

Why not take the simple path and find out what they like about their home, car, data system, etc. This is where you listen. You shut up. You do not advocate. You do not try to guide or coach them. Prospects can sense manipulation. Silence is a sign of strength and respect. You are gaining information that motivates your prospect. Your product should definitely have these features.

Many times, the prospect has not given that question any thought before.

You are helping them organize their preferences.

Question # 2 just comes naturally, without pressure. "What do you like least about your present product?"

This question will help them recognize the shortcomings of their present product - without you having to tear down their current relationship with the product or representative. Most of the prospects that I have dealt with thank me for asking the question. They say that most salespeople come and present a well-rehearsed 40-minute product presentation. They never ask questions. They basically ask that I sit patiently while they fill the room with product information. They find themselves hoping that some of what they have thrown against the wall will stick. In reality, all they have done is confuse me.

Let's see which presentation you think will result in a higher closing ratio. Which method is more time-efficient for the customer and salesperson?

Which method leads to greater customer satisfaction and referral business?

Which method will help you build a clientele and repeat business?

There is a saying in business, "You need to work smarter, not harder." Just imagine how successful a sales force would be if they employed this method. Simply put the two questions at the top of your prospect information sheet or prospect data input form.

Skipping the two questions step and going into a presentation is unprofessional. Can you imagine going to see your doctor and he didn't ask you what was wrong? He immediately prescribed penicillin-like he had for all his previous patients. Well, that is exactly what you are doing when you don't ask the two questions.

People buy products for their reasons, not yours. These questions will allow you to find out what their reason for purchase will be.

Chapter 24
Radiation And Chemo

After my head and neck surgery in 2022, I was sentenced to six and a half weeks of radiation and chemotherapy. This time, the chemotherapy was in pill form instead of infusions or injections.

The first step in radiation treatment was to be fitted with a mask. It looked remotely like a fencing mask. The screen was larger and was molded to my head so there could be no movement during the radiation treatment. Each mask is only used for one individual. This allowed the technicians to target the radiation precisely at the remaining cancer cells in my neck. The depth of proton radiation can be controlled so adjacent tissue will not be harmed.

Movement was next to impossible because you were strapped down, but fortunately, the procedure was quick. Once it started, it lasted only about two songs on the music track. I could even select my favorite songs!

We would arrive at the valet parking area of the Radiation Center Monday through Friday during half of that summer. I became familiar with everyone in the center. I decided that rather than look at this as necessary torture, I would approach this as a positive path to recovery, and everyone was my partner helping me get there.

Gradually, I became accustomed to the routine and the way the treatment was administered. I would check in at the receptionist's desk, then sit and wait to be called. A week into my treatment, I asked the receptionist her name.

"Beverly," she replied.

"That's a beautiful name. You know Beverly Hills is close to Hollywood. I'll just call you Hollywood, is that OK?"

She flashed a big smile and said, "Sure."

Obviously, not many patients had taken the time to ask her name, much less given her a nickname. Hollywood always greeted me with a smile and seemed happy to see me.

Then came the technicians. They would come into the lobby/waiting room to call the next patient. Usually, there were a handful of technicians, and one would lead you back to the radiation room, where you would remove your shirt and put on a hospital gown.

"Hi, what is your name?"

"Laura," she said.

"Are you Laura Croft?"

"No, but I dressed up like her for Halloween."

Outstanding!

Then, as the weeks spun by, our conversation was about her latest "Tombs" adventure. It made the time go by faster, and we both had fun making up our stories!

Another technician was named Andre.

"Andre, have you given up your wrestling career (Andre the Giant) to help me fight cancer?"

"Well, not exactly, but this has a higher reward than wrestling."

Another tech who joined in our flights of fancy was named Wendy.

I couldn't help myself and just had to ask her, "What is Tinkerbell really like? Word on the street is that she is still mad at you."

"She is still mad, but we are trying to reconcile."

From then on, our conversation was about how Tinkerbell was behaving. Then there was Nip. When he got me strapped in, he made sure The Rolling Stones, George Strait, or Kenny Chesney were on the music channel.

They always made sure the curtains were drawn before I removed my shirt. I had explained to them how important it was to close the drapes so as not to be confused with George Clooney. The "fencing mask" was fitted down tightly. Then came the warm blanket. My world was good.

About three weeks into the treatments, we began to plan the "Graduation Party."

I have seen different patients successfully complete their radiation treatment and "Ring the Bell."

I naturally wanted something different, and so the "Graduation Pool Party" was born.

Over the next few weeks, I began to spread the word that a pool party was planned.

Hollywood was put in charge of invitations. She needed to be cognizant of the Medical privacy laws.

Would the invitations be engraved, digital, or word of mouth? We decided word of mouth would be the most expedient.

Then, the chatter began to be about what to wear to the shindig. Hawaiian shirts were the preferred attire, of course! Sunglasses came next.

Jams (bathing suits from the 60s) and sun protective hats since many of us had cancers caused by sun damage. I accused Hollywood of only attending just to see me in a Speedo, hahaha.

Well, Graduation Day arrived. We had talked about a ukulele or steel drum band but decided not to employ one. We felt like it might stress the patients who were still going through treatment. When my wife and I arrived on my last day of treatment, we were carrying colorful Hawaiian leis.

We distributed the leis to everyone because we wanted them to have a symbol of our joy. We gave the valets leis, Hollywood and the techs were all given leis, too. Everyone was smiling and ready to celebrate Graduation.

The last treatment was completed! We marched out into the lobby and had pictures taken of my "A Team." Some of the other patients joined in the festivities. Valets really hammered it up. They all loved the recognition and that they were part of the Team.

No, we didn't actually go to a pool or hire a band. It gave us all something to talk about and allowed us to momentarily forget the stress of cancer and radiation. Pride and smiles were on everyone's face.

Chapter 25

Lessons Learned

W hen you are in a hospital or recovering at home, there is a lot of time to reminisce about events that have impacted your life.

I was lucky enough to be invited to stay with my Aunt Bonita and Uncle Bubs in Andrews, Texas, for one summer. They lived on a ranch outside of town. Uncle Bubs was the foreman of a ranch that covered 70 sections of land. One section is 640 acres. I was a twelve-year-old city boy and excited about cows, horses, and ranch life! One day, it was time for roundup.

This city boy had never heard of a roundup and had no idea what to expect. The day began early before sunrise, 4 AM.

Uncle Bubs and I got our horses and loaded them in the horse trailer behind the pickup. My introduction to West Texas conversation consisted of hearing a handful of words grunted in my direction a few times all day. My uncle was a hardworking man who just did his job and expected everyone else to work as hard as he did.

We drove for over an hour to the area we would be working. We unloaded the horses. Well, actually, I observed with big-eyed amazement while he unloaded and saddled the horses.

We mounted up, and off we rode. I had no clue where we were going or what would be expected of me.

It was still totally dark.

A little over an hour later, the first rays of sunrise began to break through the black sky.

Now that I could see my Uncle, I rode up a little closer to him and said, "Uncle Bubs, my side hurts from riding."

Without looking at me, he said, "Just ride it out, you'll be fine in a little while."

You know he was right. Twenty-five minutes later, that pain had gone away.

There is a lesson about life there, too.

Life's pain can be overcome with dogged effort if we will "just ride it out."

We finally arrived at the meeting corrals. His other neighbors met us there. I bet some of them came from 10 to 15 miles away.

Remember, a section of land is one mile by one mile. West Texas land is barren and will not support many cattle.

The land does grow every kind of thorn-producing plant known to man. Leather chaps are a necessity to keep you from getting cut up by the thorns, cactus, and mesquite bushes.

Some of his neighbors had arrived earlier and gathered the young calves into a large corral.

Without any words being said, an assembly line was formed. One cowboy on horseback would rope a calf and drag it over to a team of cowboys ready to work on him. I was told to hold the calf's hind legs while another cowboy branded him on the hip.

Each person knew his assigned job in advance.

The next step in this routine was for a cowboy with a sharp pocket knife who removed the calf's pride (testicles) and threw them in a bucket. At the opposite end of the line was a cowboy with a curved coring knife cutting the horns out of the calf. When this process was complete, the calf was released, wondering what had just happened to him.

The next calf was roped and drug to the waiting cowboys and was quickly processed through the same efficient procedure.

I am going to guess that my eyes were the size of dinner plates. This was a completely foreign world to the City boy. My first attempt at holding the back legs of a calf being branded sent me flying across the corral.

Calves kick hard when being branded. The smell of burning hair and flesh left me gasping for air.

After witnessing the branding and surgery at the rear end, it was time to move to the front. My next job was to hold the calf's head. I had learned from experience to hold on tightly as the calf was processed.

This new job found me going eyeball to eyeball with each new calf. They each seemed to ask, "Why are you doing this?" or say, "Ooooh! I really don't like that." If looks could kill, I knew who would be first.

The roundup was complete by late afternoon. The calves were released to their mothers and were quickly cleaned up by them. Cowboys waved their goodbyes and thank you to all that had helped out.

Bubs and I rode back to where we parked the horse trailer. We were proud of the day's work and starved by that time.

When we arrived back at the ranch, we unsaddled the horses, brushed them down, and then put them back in the coral. I left Uncle Bubs at the barn and raced to the house for dinner.

My Aunt Bonita was a great cook, and I couldn't wait to see what she had made. I'll never forget, as I came busting through the front door, she said, "Don't come into this house with your hat and spurs on or No Dinner for you!"

This was a different world with different rules, but I was really hungry and wanted to please my aunt and uncle.

To this day, I don't feel comfortable wearing a Western hat or spurs indoors!

*****

Fran and Eddie Chiles were a power couple in Ft Worth. They were involved in everything in the city and state. They were always trying to make our city a better place to live and work.

Eddie had started his oil field service company with one truck. After years of hard work, he had grown it to a giant public oil well servicing company. He was the true American success story.

Eddie was a no-nonsense person. He wasn't accepting any excuses. If he saw a problem, he would jump in and work on solving it. He had bumper stickers that read, "If you don't have an oil well, get one; you'll Love doing business with Western Company."

Eddie was the perfect example of "One man can make a difference.

If there is something you don't like, he would say, "Don't stay mad. Get up and do something about it."

He produced radio advertisements explaining his frustration with government inefficiencies. He even carried it further by creating bumper stickers that read, "I'm mad, too, Eddie."

Fran, who was his perfect partner, looked after the details of their marriage. She made sure that all the behind-the-scenes workers were always recognized at dinners and fundraisers. She made a special effort to recognize the kitchen workers, waiters, and any others who would be striving to make the night successful.

Fran watched for even the smallest of details. One night at a charity fundraiser, she came over to me and said, "Mac, you have your name tag on wrong."

I didn't know that there was a right way or a wrong way to wear a name tag. I had stuck it neatly on my left breast coat pocket.

"Here, let me fix that. It goes on the right lapel of your coat. You see, Mac, most people are right-handed. That way, when you meet someone, as they shake your hand, they can see your name tag and maintain eye contact. Lesson learned.

*****

Frank Kent: "If you are not making mistakes, you are not trying. Become involved in your community and make it better."

Willard Pratt: "If you are going to be a fly, don't be a little housefly; be a Great Big Green Horsefly!"

"Honesty is not the best policy, it is the only policy. Hard, honest, intelligent effort is always rewarded."

My Aunt Lou: "Your table manners are a reflection of your parents and your aunt."

Mother: "Someone is always watching you. It may only be yourself."

Franklin Delano Roosevelt: "Be sincere, be brief, and be seated." (in speeches)

Francis Bacon: "Knowledge is Power"

Children need boundaries so they know they are loved.

The journey of 1,000 miles is taken with the first step.

The Best Investment is in yourself.

There is a price at which everything will sell.

You only get out of life what you put into it.

We all have different passions. Our degree of satisfaction with our passion will be measured by how much time and resources we commit. A casual effort will garner very little satisfaction. Full commitment will provide great satisfaction and may earn you chairmanship of your endeavor. Let your passion leave this world a better place than it was when you found it.

Dad: "Treat every gun as if it was loaded. Always keep Guns pointed away from people. The job is never done until the floor is mopped after the restaurant is closed for the night."

Senator Phil Gramm: "You always tax what you want less of."

Dean Cozine, High school history teacher, "The Best form of government is the least. Rasputin was a hard person to kill."

Holt Hickman's was an extremely successful businessman. I asked him what his first car was. He said it was Model T chicken coop – that he paid $5 for. He said he had to shovel out a ton of chicken fertilizer before he could sit down. Holt was a very successful businessman and was not afraid of hard work.

Willard Pratt: "Fear not the big boss. Typically, the higher you climb in an organization, the nicer the people are. Remember, they didn't get to the top being mean or nasty."

THERE ARE ONLY TWO THINGS THAT WILL CHANGE A PERSON. THEY ARE THE BOOKS YOU READ AND THE PEOPLE YOU MEET.

Chapter 26
Duck Hunting

Another time during radiation, I was remembering back to my college days. A group of us were sitting around the fraternity house talking about duck hunting.

"Yeah, I went last year and hardly even saw a bird."

"That's too bad… We got our limit almost every time we went out!"

"Well, it's just great being out on the lake with the dogs, fresh air, and in nature."

"At sunrise, just as the sun starts lighting up the morning sky, the ducks start flying. It is just a beautiful sight."

"Hey, the season opens next week. We can go out to my hunting lease on Lake Granbury. I have had good luck every year there. I just finished working the blinds, and they are good to go."

John, our fraternity brother from New York City, had been listening intently. He hadn't said a word but had a very interested look on his face.

"John, have you ever been duck hunting?" "Not exactly. Actually, never."

"Why don't you go with us? I think you will love it!" "That would be great, but I don't even have a gun."

77

"Don't worry about that, we'll fix you up. You'll need waders, a hat and warm jacket, gloves, and a license. We have a week to get you ready, and we can get you all outfitted. This will be a new adventure for you."

"Gosh, guys, thanks for including me."

That week flew by with eager anticipation. John was now geared up with a shotgun, shells, ski jacket, waders, and a federal duck stamp license. We were on a road trip to Granbury.

We all stayed at one of the brother's homes. We slept lightly, expecting a Big Day on the lake.

We were up early and out the door by 4 AM. Everyone was eager for the adventure, and we loaded all of our gear into the duck blind boats and headed out to the blinds in the shallows of the lake.

Since this was John's first duck hunt, we took him out to the first and always Best Blind. We dropped him off, checking to make sure he had everything he needed: a Coffee thermos, gun and shells, gloves, and a flashlight.

"Wait till sunrise to start shooting," we advised. Happy Hunting. We will be back to pick you up later this morning after everyone has gotten their limit of ducks."

Putt, putt, putt. Off we went, dropping each hunter off at his duck blind. Everyone was situated in a blind by 5 AM. Some might not consider this fun, but sharing your time with the man above, in the world He built, is exhilarating. Watching the duck dogs (Labrador Retrievers) work picking up the downed birds is beautiful. They enjoy the sport as much as the hunters or maybe more!

The world stops churning for this moment in time, and you can feel the tension leave your body.

Sunrise comes, and the action begins. Birds began flying over, and shots rang out. A couple of birds fall from the sky and splash down. Just as the birds hit the water, the dogs go into action. Jake is the biggest and fastest of the dogs. Splash! He hits the water, followed closely by Sadie. Jake paddles out and retrieves a green head (a Mallard). Sadie has to swim out a little further to pick up her Red head duck.

Watching the dogs work is like watching ballet on water.

Most hunters will say that to witness a good dog work is half the fun.

The shooting stopped as the sun had gotten higher in the sky. It was time to pack it in. The duck blind pickup began putt, putt, putt.

As we picked up each hunter, he would begin telling us about his hunting success. Everyone wanted to share his experience with the group!

There were many varieties of ducks taken that day.

There were Widgeon, Teal, Merganser, Wood Duck, and Mallards. Andy said, "As good as my hunt was, I don't think I heard John shoot."

Gregg, who was in the duck blind with Andy, chimed in, "I don't think I heard him shooting either. Maybe we were just too far away. I got my limit, and it was sure fun to watch Jake work!"

"Well, load up the boat, and let's go get the others. Make room for Jake." Putt, putt, putt.

We pulled up to the blind to get Steve and Louis, who were ready to tell their stories and hear about everyone else's morning.

"How did you all do?"

Steve had a big smile on his face and said, "I got my limit in the first hour."

Louis joined in with, "It took me a bit longer to get my limit. Guess I'm a bit rusty and didn't lead the ducks enough at first. Sadie did find all the ducks and was super on the retrieval!"

"OK, load up, and let's go get John. How do you think he did today?"

Steve commented that. "It sure seemed quiet over there. Don't think I heard him shoot all morning. Of course, I could have been focused on the ducks and Sadie."

"You know, come to think of it, I don't recall any shots coming from his blind. Louis agreed.

"What do you think? Maybe the ducks just didn't get over to that part of the lake this year."

"I don't know. It has always been the best spot every year. Or maybe his gun was jammed. Well, hop in, and let's go see what's up." Putt, putt, putt.

We putt, putt right through what seemed like a Walt Disney movie as the ducks were flushed into the air ahead of the boat. Ducks were everywhere. All kinds of ducks and all colors of ducks.

We pulled up to John's blind, and Andy yelled out, "How did you do?" Ashamed, John confessed that, "I didn't get any."

Steve asked, "Was your gun jammed?"

John answered, "No, I just didn't see any ducks."

"Well, we just drove through an ocean of ducks getting to your blind." Steve declared.

Surprised, John said, "Those were ducks? I thought ducks were all white."

This brought a roar of laughter from the hunters.

This was the day that we all learned that perspective is determined by exposure. The only ducks that John had ever seen were the white domesticated kind at the public parks in New York City! We also learned not to assume anything, even though it was second nature to us. We also began to understand that life is better when shared with friends!

Chapter 27

Yellow Rolls Royce

Tuesday.

There she is, the Valet Cashier., This is one of the most thankless, monotonous jobs in the hospital system. The only time they are noticed is when a patient's car can't be found, or it takes too long to find and deliver the patient's car.

"Yes, ma'am, we would like to get our car. It is Ticket #619, a Yellow Rolls Royce."

"Well, let me pull it up," all the time with an expression on her face that says, "This guy is full of baloney."

"Honey, that ticket is for a red Cadillac. Is that what you meant?"

"Actually, I'm pretty sure we drove the Rolls today."

Smiling, she said, "If you come back tomorrow, we will have that car for you."

She read me like a book, and now it was time to have fun.

"We are not due back until Friday. Could you hold it for me?" I asked, grinning as we were having fun with this teasing banter.

"Oh no! I can't be responsible for a car that nice," she said, almost bent over laughing.

"Well, it looks like I'll have to struggle to get by with the Cadillac," I said, waving goodbye with a Big Smile on my face.

I asked her, "What is your name?"

"Betty."

"Why, that is a lovely name. My grandmother was named Betty."

I can't wait to hear what she says Friday when I drop by her desk and tell her I'm here to pick up my Yellow Rolls Royce.

If laughter is good for the soul, it certainly can't hurt the healing process. Friday.

I have just finished my neck surgery check-up at the hospital. The doctor is extremely pleased with the results and healing process. I must try to start using some of my body parts that were operated on.

We checked out of the doctor's clinic and set future appointments. Next, we headed down to pick up our car at the Valet stand. Let the fun begin.

We waited patiently in line to turn in our tickets and pay like the other 'normal' customers.

Betty, the valet stand cashier, is focused on the customer just in front of us and hasn't had a chance to look up.

I say, "Ticket number 741, a Yellow Rolls Royce."

Betty jerks her head up to see who is requesting a Yellow Rolls Royce.

"I know you from earlier this week!" she says with a big smile. Looks like she has been planning this moment.

"So, did you drive the Yellow Rolls Royce today?"

"I sure did," I said in a quite confident manner.

"Well, that will be $20," she said.

"Now, hold on. This sign on the front of this desk says $5 to valet park."

"Yeah, but you are driving a Yellow Rolls Royce! Come to think of it, maybe the charge should be $50!" she is bent over the desk, laughing hard.

I am impressed with her wit and interaction. This is fun for both of us.

"Maybe I ought to charge you for parking my Yellow Rolls Royce!"

We are both laughing so hard we hurt.

"I just remembered, I drove the Cadillac today. Thanks for all you do. I'll be back with my Rolls."

Kind of hard to say, but I am looking forward to my next doctor's appointment. I can't wait to see what Betty has planned for me.

One week later. We have just finished with my check-up and are patiently waiting in the valet ticket line. Our turn to pay arrives.

Betty looks up and, immediately recognizes me, and says, "Here comes trouble! I mean trouble," she is smiling from ear to ear.

My wife agrees with her, saying, "Yeah, the first thing I see every morning is Trouble."

I say, "Ticket number 4107, a Yellow Rolls Royce." Now, she is ready. "That will be $100. Surely anyone that can afford a Rolls Royce can afford a $100 parking ticket."

"Well, usually when I pay that much for parking, they wash and gas my car. Did you perform those expected services? Well, my guess would be no. So, I will not pick up my car until those services are performed." We are all bent over laughing and having fun.

"We will be sure to have it washed next time you are here, but you will have to put in your own gas!" she said as we walked out the door to our car. I can't wait to find out the fun comments she will have next time.

Chapter 28

Private Room, Champagne, Oysters, Roses

T he cancer has migrated to the right side of my neck. I have had the surgery and now it is time for 6 ½ weeks of radiation. When checking in with the receptionist person at the front desk you are always asked your name. I have responded, "Mac Churchill."

"And your date of birth?"

I answer quite routinely.

This routine questioning goes on for five more days as I receive treatment. They now know who I am and I haven't found anybody that is willing to impersonate me or take the radiation treatments for me.

There is a new girl on the front desk today!

"What's your name sir?" she asks quite professionally.

I answer, "George Clooney," as if it was my real name.

She studies the screen.

Then she asks, "What time was your appointment?"

Innocently, I answer, "9:30."

After searching for a few more moments, I tell her she may want to look under Churchill.

"Yes, here it is. You are checked in. You can go back to the dressing room."

Now, after several check-ins, when I return, they greet me with the big smiles and say, "Good morning, Mr. Clooney."

This banter goes on for about a week.

Now it's time to add an extra ingredient.

"Good morning, is my private room ready?" we are playing the game and having fun.

Taking a moment to process what I just said, she quickly responds, "Why of course, just as you requested."

Of course, there is no private room but it makes check-in fun and brings a conspiratorial smile.

This private room ruse goes on for a few days. When I show up for my treatment and ask, "Is my private room ready?" she responds, "Why, of course. Mr. Clooney! And the champagne is iced down, as you ordered," is the quick professional reply with a happy smile. Wow, this girl is quite clever and witty.

Upon leaving my radiation treatment, I thank her for the initiative in having the champagne iced down in a bucket by the radiation table.

The next treatment date has arrived. Upon entering the lobby to the radiation center, I am greeted with, "Good morning, Mr. Clooney."

"Good morning, is my private room ready? With champagne?" I ask. Giving me a smile and a wink, she says, "Of course, it is ready."

I head back to the dressing area and put on the hospital gown. Shortly thereafter, Heather "Locklear" comes to escort me to the treatment room. "Is my private room ready? Is the champagne iced down?"

"Yes, all of it, is as you requested," she said with a proud smile. This was all so out of the 'norm' of regular radiation treatment, that she loved playing along.

I was ready for the treatment and as I hopped up on the table the girls noticed my soxx. "Are those your Happy Soxx?"

"They sure are — those are Toucans with big yellow beaks."

"Those are cool. I can see how they would make you feel happy when you wear them," she said smiling.

They began taping my neck and eyelid. "Hey, you are not going to use that Brazilian wax tape like the last time, are you?"

"No, no just regular gauze tape. Why?" she replied with a quizzical smile.

"Heck, last time I lost an eyebrow!" I said to, Sam I am. "They used Brazilian waxing tape."

Banter reduces stress for all involved and makes the time pass. "Hah, hahaha, no, you'll be fine - just lie back and listen to Jimmy Buffett." Another successful treatment was completed. "Thanks, that treatment only took two songs to complete. I'll see you tomorrow." I said as I exited to get dressed.

I waved at the receptionist on the way out. She motioned me over. "We will have some oysters to go with the champagne in your room tomorrow!" Wow! She is really having fun with this and so am I "That would be perfect! By the way, the champagne was chilled to perfection. See you tomorrow."

When I checked in the next morning, she said "Good morning, Mr. Clooney."

"Good morning! Is my private room ready? And is the champagne chilled?"

"Yes sir, and you will love the fresh oysters we had flown in this morning." She is quite proud of the addition that she has made to the witty wordplay.

"Wow! I have never experienced such thoughtful service! You have anticipated my every need."

Arriving the next morning I was greeted with, "Good morning Mr. Clooney."

"Good morning!" I replied. 'Is everything ready in my private room?"

"Oh, yes sir, we have your champagne iced down and we have your Blue Point oysters on ice!" This is all said just loud enough for everyone in the waiting room to overhear. Most everyone looked up just to see if George Clooney was really standing there.

I went to the dressing room and changed into the open back hospital gown. Then Foo man Cho showed up to take me back for treatment. "Foo how did your Memorial Day weekend go?" I asked.

"Oh super, I had my brothers over and we barbecued some ribs," he proudly shared.

"What kind of work do your brothers do?" I asked.

"They are all in the oncology medical field," he proudly said.

"OK, let's get this mask on you. I'll get Pat Green cranked up for you in just a moment." Foo said in full control.

"OK, that would be outstanding," I replied.

The next week I was introduced to a new 'A Team member.' "What is your name?"

"Antoinette," is her unengaging reply. See most patients don't want any conversation. Just shoot me with radiation and get out as fast as possible. I have found that simply treating people as important really increases the care you receive. The place to start is their name. I will immediately try to word associate with their name.

"Do you mind if I call you Marie Antoinette, like the Queen of France?"

"No, that would be fine," she replied with a regal smile. The next day she was part of my treatment team. I said, "Good morning Marie Antoinette?" You could have knocked her over with a feather. She had a surprised look on her face that said very few people had ever acknowledged her before.

Unfortunately, too many caregivers are treated as another inconvenience. Just one more hurdle to jump over on their treatment path.

The final week is at hand. The final preparations have been made for the Yodeling Pickle Choir. The receptionist motions me over as I was headed out to retrieve my car.

"Yes, the oysters were chilled to perfection. The older vintage of champagne was such a nice touch!" I bragged about our mythical room service.

"Well, what I called you over for was to let you know that we will have a dozen red roses in your room tomorrow," she announced excitedly.

"How can I thank you? That is just so thoughtful." I said very overwhelmed with the kind thought.

Once outside, I noticed that my car was parked by the front door. This had been happening regularly for the last several weeks. This would save us time. No waiting around while they hunted for it in the garage. Our valet had become quite familiar with us coming Monday through Friday for weeks now. My treatments only took a few minutes. We had taken the time to find out his name and some things that were going on in his life. He treated us with his special kindness by parking the car up front.

Yes, he was a member of the 'Pool Party Graduation' and had his picture made with the rest of the 'A Team.'

Upon arrival at the radiation center, I was greeted with "Good morning, Mr. Clooney!"

"Good morning! Is everything ready in my Private room?"

"Yes, sir! Your private room is ready with champagne, oysters, and a dozen red roses!"

This easy-going exchange and joking has made six- and one-half weeks of chemo and radiation pass quickly. Each visit was curiously fun to see what the team members would come up with next. We could all look forward to the fun dialog each visit would bring. All the while, my treatments were being administered, we were planning our 'Yodeling Pickle Choir graduation ceremony.

Chapter 29

Yodeling Pickle Choir

W hile all the fun conversations about private rooms and champagne were taking place, important issues needed to be addressed. The graduation party needed to be planned.

This Graduate radiation degree is going to require some real imagination. How do you follow the very successful graduation Pool

Party? One of my friends came to the rescue. I have constantly threatened to yodel at dinners or birthday parties.

My friend Jim found a novelty, "Yodeling Pickle." Yeah, that's right, a plastic pickle that yodels. I can work with this. I think that we can build a Yodeling Pickle Choir. Naturally, we will have to have tryouts. Will we have solo singing spots? How many practices should we have? Should we have uniforms for the choir? What kind of musical accompaniment should we have with a yodeling pickle? A successful choir doesn't just happen until these and many other questions can be dealt with.

The first day of treatment arrived. I checked in and waited to be called to go back and receive treatment. I was called and then taken back to a changing room and then shown to the patient waiting room. I arrived and joined two other patients waiting their turn. One had stage 4 colon cancer, and the other had neck cancer, but no surgery had been required.

After I had finished my radiation treatment, I returned to the waiting/dressing room. The fellows that I had left in the waiting room were still waiting for their turn. They looked pretty grim. I dressed quickly and returned to the waiting room. "Hey, fellas, it looks like you guys could use a laugh. Have you ever seen a Yodeling Pickle?"

I reached into my clothes bag and pulled out a 6-inch-long plastic green pickle. I hit the play button, and it began to yodel. They were at first hesitant, then curious, and of course they were still not sure what I was holding in my hand. They lit up when they realized that I just wanted to give them each a moment of silly, innocent fun. Smiles filled the room. One of the men said, "Hey, let's hear that again!"

I got the feeling that this was the first thing that they had laughed at in a long time. I left the room with them, smiling and escaping the reality of pain and uncertainty for a few moments.

The next day, I was entering the waiting room and ran into the fella with stage 4 cancer. He was headed back to get his radiation treatment. He looked up and recognized me and said, "You still got that pickle?" He had a smile from ear to ear. Wow! Moments like that make it all worthwhile. The six and half weeks of chemotherapy and radiation marched along fairly quickly. The therapy techs brought fellow therapists by to see and hear the yodeling pickle. Everyone seems to leave with a smile after witnessing the Incredible Yodeling Pickle. I had heartfelt discussions about the Yodeling Pickle Choir, formerly known as the "Cucumber Choir." We needed serious questions answered.

Would we need musical accompaniment?

Should we have a champagne reception after our performance? Should we sign autographs?

How should we get invitations to our close family members so they can witness this truly historic event?

These were all important questions that needed to be addressed if we were going to have a successful event.

Everyone's input was considered. Talks of midnight meetings were discussed but quickly dismissed.

Finally, the last day of radiation arrived. The treatment was administered. I jumped up and put my Hawaiian shirt on. I herded my team and the neighboring therapists to the front lobby. We were joined by the receptionist and the valet parkers.

My trophy wife lined us all up. She then passed out yodeling pickles to all the choir members. Everyone began tuning their pickles up. Then, on the count of 3, we all played our pickles (almost) in unison. Picture perfect!

Hahaha! Great fun was enjoyed by all as we took a group photo to memorialize my "A Team." They had all been a big part of my fight against cancer. Maybe this Yodeling Pickle exercise put a smile on their face and some momentary relief from their daily stress.

Life's challenges are always easier to face with a smile!

WE CANNOT CONTROL WHAT HAPPENS TO US IN LIFE, WE CAN ONLY CONTROL HOW WE REACT.

Chapter 30
Ancestors

Well, it's been a year since my last Mohs surgery. That's a total of 3 Mohs to the skull surgeries in 5 years.

I asked the plastic surgeon that was installing my Integra patches over my operation site "if he had done a 23 and me test ?"

"Why do you ask ?"

He has been treating me for years now and gotten wise to me.

"Just curious" I said with a completely straight face.

"Actually, I haven't taken one of those tests. Mac have you taken one ?"

"Yes, I have. Found out that I am English and Scottish. This of course was no big revelation. It also said that way back there I had some Neanderthal bloodlines. I think though that you ought to do a test."

"Why do you say that ?"

"The way that you have had to cut on my head. I think that you would find that some of your blood lines were Apache Indian."

"And what makes you think, I don't live in a tepee?" He said with a very mysterious expressionless face.

This caused me to pause ever so briefly and say to myself, "naw he's kidding, right?"

Noticing my almost imperceptible pause, he grinned. He knew that he had finally turned the tables on me.

We both broke out into belly laughs at the same time. This allowed us both to escape the natural stress that comes from medical procedures.

I think laughter helps the healing process. Next time you are having a procedure try it. Prove me wrong. They may commit you but, at least you will have a smile on your face.

Chapter 31
The Psychology of Color

The Healing Power of Color in Life and Fashion

Cancer is a journey, a battle where mental resilience and emotional strength often play as significant a role as medical interventions. One surprising ally in this fight can be found in something as simple yet profound as color. The hues we wear and the colors that surround us can profoundly influence our mood, mindset ,and overall well-being, especially during challenging times like a cancer diagnosis.

The Psychology of Color

Colors have the unique ability to evoke feelings and memories. This phenomenon, known as color psychology, suggest that different colors can inspire various emotional responses. For those battling cancer, harnessing this power can be a transformative experience.

Warm Colors

Shades of red, orange, and yellow are often associated with warmth and energy. Wearing vibrant reds can boost confidence and assertiveness, while sunny yellows can uplift your spirits, reminding you of brighter days. During my treatment, I found that wearing bold colors made me feel strong and ready to face each day, as if I were wearing armor against my adversities.

Cool Colors

Blues and greens tend to evoke feelings of calmness and tranquility.

When anxiety loomed large, slipping into a soft blue shirt or finding a quite area with plants helped create peaceful sanctuary. These colors reminded me to breathe deeply and live in the present. This allows you to momentarily set aside your worries and be thankful for the present.

Personalizing your Palette

Finding your personal palette can be an enriching experience. It's more than just fashion, it's about expression. I began to build a wardrobe filled with colors that resonated with my emotions and experiences. Each piece had its value as a symbol of my journey.

Creating a Colorful Environment

Beyond clothing, the colors in our living spaces can also contribute to our emotional well-being. I transformed my home into a vibrant retreat filled with vibrant artwork and colorful cushions. Each room became a canvas of expression, filled with hues that reflected my journey.

Mindful Spaces

I designated a Corner of my living room as mindful space. This became my sanctuary for meditation and reflection, a place I could pause and deflect with my inner self. The calming colors tend to create a sense of safety and reassurance, reminding me that I was not alone in my struggle.

The Future A Colorful Outlook

As I navigated through treatment, I learned that embracing colors in my clothing and environment wasn't just a method of coping it became a celebration of life. Dressing with color daily became a statement of hope and resilience, a reminder that that joy could coexist with the struggle.

Add color to your fight and put a smile on someone's face.

Chapter 32

The Texas Ear

I t's been five years and several surgeries since I lost 75% of my left ear to cancer.

So, at the urging of my wife, we have scheduled an appointment with Mosaic Prosthetics, a company that makes prosthetic ears, noses, etc. I am guessing that my wife was tired of me scaring little kids with only one ear.

Upon arrival, we were welcomed with open arms by Becky, the receptionist.

After a short conversation, we were given the usual stack of forms to fill out and sign. Strangely, there wasn't a list of choices as to what kind of ear I preferred. Focus! Just finish the forms. All signed and dated.

"Mac, tell me about those colorful socks you have on," Becky said.

"Yes, these are my Happy Soxx. I wear them as a flag in my fight against cancer. You know Cancer Hates Color. So, every morning when I put on my colorful socks, I smile because I am armed to take on whatever challenge lies ahead.

"Well, I have on my Happy Soxx, too," Becky said, revealing her socks. I wear these colorful socks to fight the blah and mundane."

"Isn't that a picture of a dog?" I asked curiously.

"Yes, that's a picture of my dog," she answered with a big smile.

"Well, that's Super Cool! I'm always glad to welcome another member into the army fighting cancer," I said with a welcoming hug.

The other two girls in the office were listening to our chatter and commented that they liked the idea.

We proceeded to the modeling room. They had me sit down in a medical chair, where they began explaining the next steps in the procedure and what to expect. They took measurements and examined the scar tissue that would be covered with my new ear.

Then, they began mixing a concoction to make a mold of my right ear. When the goop was properly mixed, they began applying it to my right ear. They intended to make a mold so that they could reverse engineer my left ear. The entire process was quite interesting and painless.

After about 30 minutes, the mold was removed and checked for imperfections.

They continued to make small alterations until they were satisfied with the mold impression. We were scheduled to return in three weeks.

We arrived at Mosaic Prosthetics at noon for our appointment and were warmly greeted by Becky, who made sure I signed the next set of forms. What she really came in for was to join the other girls who were showing off their Happy Soxx. They all had smiles, and we took a picture showing off our socks.

This was Becky's day off, but she came in to share the Positive Spirit that Color and Happy Soxx bring. Becky also wanted to tell me about an inspiring annual retreat she and her girlfriends go on in the summers.

Becky handed us off to Allison and Ashley, who took me back to the chair in the fitting room. They produced my new left ear and began perfecting it even further.

`They began to shape, poke, and prod the ear. I don't think they thought it was dead yet. They went back and forth to the lab, working until they achieved the perfect fit.

This entire process is a miracle of technology and artistry.

While all this fitting was going on, we talked about what kind of ear I wanted.

"Well, what do you envision? What kind of ear do you want?" Allison asked.

Boxers call it leading with your chin. Way to tee it up for me, Allison! Since it is so hot in the summer, I want the "Texas Ear "that comes with a remote control, which will allow me to move my ear to fan myself lightly in the hot summertime.

I also need a button on the remote that will allow my ear to swat a fly or mosquito. I would also like a button that will wiggle my ear to entertain the grandkids . Finally, I need a hole for a pirate's earring in case I have to fill in for Johnny Depp as Jack Sparrow in the movies. "

I said this all very seriously, tongue-in-cheek.

"If we put the Texas Ear on you, I think it would be a good idea to watch that remote, or your wife might whack you with it!" Allison said jokingly. We spent the next few minutes discussing what other buttons we should add to the remote. Lots of fun and laughter was had by all.

We spent an hour and a half driving to our noon appointment at Mosaic Prosthetics in McKinney, Texas, and around two hours at the appointment. When we finished the fitting, we were famished and asked about a nice restaurant nearby.

They recommended Urban Grill and Wine Bar, just a few blocks away. The restaurant specialized in wonderful Italian pasta dishes and a great wine selection. It made our hunger disappear in such a delightful manner. We celebrated my new ear and a step toward "Normal". We even toasted one of our favorite California wine makers, the late Josh Jensen of Calera Wines, with a glass of his Chardonnay.

Let me reminisce a moment and remember when we were in San Francisco and met Josh Jensen. We had arrived without reservations at our favorite restaurant in San Francisco - Gary Danko. Naturally, they were full and had no available table for us.

They offered to have us wait in the bar for the next available seating. We knew it would be worth the wait.

The bar was semi-circular, with some guests seated at the bar and others standing behind them. We became some of those standing behind the lucky ones who found a seat at the bar. Because the restaurant was packed, I had to worm my way into the crowd. Reaching over and placing my order was a chore.

The fellow that I reached past said, "Hey, it's tough getting through here. Why don't I just hand them to you when your order is ready?"

"That would be great! Thank you ." I said gratefully.

The drinks arrived, and he turned around and handed them to us. "Where are you from?" Josh asked, recognizing our accents.

"We are from Fort Worth, Texas. And where are you from?" I asked loudly to speak over the noise around the bar.

"Oh, me? I live a little South of here," he replied, as I sensed there was more to the story.

One chair opened up at the bar next to Josh. I quickly moved my wife into the seat, and I stood between Josh and Lu Jo. The conversation continued.

"So, you are from Ft Worth. Do you know the Bass family?" Josh asked as we began to find out about each other.

"Yes, they are a very prominent family in Fort Worth. We run in different circles. How do you know them?" I queried.

Then we were off to the races with his life story. Josh met the Basses at Yale University when they were students. It was at Yale where he developed a taste for Chardonnay wine. He graduated and went straight to the Montrachet region of France to discover the secrets of making the finest Chardonnay.

He worked for several vineyards, starting at the bottom. He tried to learn as much as he could about every phase of growing, harvesting, and producing grapes. He concluded that a limestone rock formation was absolutely essential for outstanding Chardonnay. He found a limestone formation just North of San Francisco that was almost the same as the famous French area. There, he built his vineyard, Calera - home of some of the world's finest Chardonnay.

I just had to ask Josh about the jacket he was wearing that night. I had never seen one like it before. It was a fine black wool that was perfectly tailored. Josh was probably a little over six feet tall and fit.

The lapels, pocket flaps, and lower edges were all outlined with silver studs. The outstanding feature was on the inside lining. He opened his jacket, and inside, on the front right side, it had been personally autographed by Gianni Versace himself. It was one of a kind, custom-made for Josh!

We returned a couple of weeks later to Mosaic Prosthetics for the final fitting of my new ear. Ashley spent half an hour color-matching the new ear to my complexion. She said she can even add freckles to match a client's skin! She schooled us in the proper care and application/removal process and wished us well!

We all wanted to have a group photo showing off my miracle new ear and showing off our Happy Soxx. Don't you love Becky's Panda Soxx? We all started our day with a smile when we put on our Happy Soxx that morning.

The final fitting went well. Now, I won't be scaring little kids!

The grandkids couldn't quite figure out what was different about me. Now, with my new ear, I'm waiting on the call from Hollywood to fill in for Johnny Depp or George Clooney.

Add color to your life, and make someone smile.

Chapter 33

Cancer Hates Color

W ell, it's been 10 years since I started on this journey of fighting cancer. It's been 18 months since my last neck surgery for cancer. This was followed by six weeks of radiation and The Yodeling Pickle Choir.

It's been one year since my battle with shingles (yes, I had a shingles shot).

I am relating this to you not to get sympathy, but to say the journey may be long.

And, at times, desperate. Don't despair. Keep your chin up and become a pillar of strength. Wear your "Magic Colors."

Cancer Hates Color!

Color represents hope and an inner fight not to give up. Finding your personal expression can be an enriching experience. I am recommending that you add color to your wardrobe. Not a circus clown outfit, but rather something tasteful. Clothing that resonates with your personality. Each piece should become a flag of defiance and put an inward smile on your face.

Each day, I dress and put on my armor, sliding on my Happy Soxx and colorful shirt or sweater. I start the day with a smile. I am emitting positive vibes. When I go to my appointments, the nurses want to know what I am wearing that day. They are always checking out my Happy Soxx.

Many times, the nurses will comment that they saw that I was coming in that day so that they wore their Happy Soxx. This always produces a smile and solidarity in the fight against cancer. I now have many friends that are wearing Happy Soxx and who have added color to their lives and wardrobes. They don't have cancer, but it makes them smile and feel positive.

Cancer hates Color when a community gathers to fight cancer, and everyone is wearing a color. This sea of color shows a solidarity and recognition of the evil that cancer presents. Different types of cancer are represented by various colors. Here are some of the most common:

- Pink: Breast cancer
- Light Blue: Prostate cancer
- Teal: Ovarian cancer
- Lavender: All cancers (general awareness)
- Orange: Leukemia
- Gold: Childhood cancer
- Green: Liver cancer
- Purple: Pancreatic cancer
- Red: AIDS awareness, but also used for certain cancers like kidney cancer
- Yellow: Wristband, Lance Armstrong, hope and perseverance for cancer patients; Live Strong

Each color serves as a symbol to raise awareness and support for research, treatment, and prevention efforts.

Wear color to show defiance to cancer and become an inspiration to others fighting cancer. Start with your "Happy Soxx" and a smile every morning.

Chapter 34
Between The Ears

Eleven years ago this journey began. Chemotherapy, Blood Draws, Blood Transfusions, Bone Marrow Transplant, Mohs Surgeries, Neck Surgeries, Shingles, CT Scans, Radiation Treatments and all mixed with a few hospital stays.

We all have adversity in our lives. Adversity is inevitable. It can strike in many forms a lost job, health issues, or even the quiet yet relentless whisper of self-doubt. Each challenge presents a choice: to succumb to despair or to rise, transform, and emerge stronger on the other side. This chapter should help you harness the power of adversity, turning it into a crucible for personal growth.

My personal motto in dealing with adversity: *"I want to come out of this situation better than I went into it."*

This allows me to focus on the outcome and not the adversity . How can I improve myself while dealing with this problem?

But before we can navigate adversity, we must first understand it. Adversity is not merely a set of unfortunate events, it is a teacher, albeit a harsh one. It provides us with the opportunity to reassess our values, beliefs, and goals. I know that many times I felt like someone was standing in the back of a truck throwing out obstacles for me to jump over or avoid.

Shift to the positive: instead of viewing challenges as obstacles, consider them as stepping stones. A powerful technique to achieve this shift is the practice of reframing. This involves changing the way you look at a situation. For example, a hospital stay may allow you to read or reconnect with family or friends. You probably never found the time to connect with them while working or juggling children.

Research has shown that Resilience is not an innate trait but a skill that can be cultivated. Here are some ideas to enhance your resilience:

1) **Build a Support Network.** Surround yourself with positive individuals who will encourage growth. Share your struggles with them: vulnerability can strengthen bonds.

2) **Practice Self-Compassion:** Treat yourself with kindness during difficult times. Acknowledge that it is okay to feel pain and that struggles are part of the human experience.

3) **Set Realistic Goals:** Breakdown your challenges into manageable tasks. Achieving small goals can provide a sense of accomplishment. Don't try to eat the elephant all in one bite .

4) **Embrace Change:** Accept that change is a constant in life. The more you resist it, the more difficult adversity will feel. Embrace change as an opportunity for growth.

5) **Practice being in the present.**

Ultimately, the key to coming out stronger on the other side of adversity lies in adopting a Positive Mindset. This Positive Mindset embraces challenges, persists in the face of setbacks, and effort is the key to success. By believing you can grow from every challenge, you add strength to yourself to face whatever the new challenge comes your way. When sitting in patient waiting rooms, I notice that many patients are in worse shape than myself. This observation makes me snap out of any momentary self-pity and refocus on the positive. A Positive Mindset can have profound effects on our physical and mental well-being. Patients who practice gratitude and positive thinking often experience lower levels of stress and anxiety. Make the most of your waiting time by refocusing on the positive and being in the present.

Being in the present moment, often referred to as mindfulness, allows us to fully engage with life as it unfolds. The practice encourages us to let go of distractions and worries about the future or regrets about the past. This allows us to have a greater appreciation of Now.

When we immerse ourselves in the Here and Now, we can savor simple pleasures - like the taste of our food, the warmth of the sun, or the laughter of a grandchild, or the smile of a caregiver. This will transform ordinary moments into pleasurable experiences.

Additionally living in the present fosters a sense of connection with ourselves and others. Being in the present means that we must become more compassionate and more empathetic. It is that we are more attuned to the feelings and needs of others.

Ultimately, Living in the Moment allows us to live more authentically and enjoy life more completely.

I have found that maybe the ultimate form of Living in the Moment is prayer. Praying in the moment can be a deeply transformative experience. Praying allows me to connect with my thoughts and feelings in a profound way. Whether it's during a significant life event, such as a wedding, a birth, or medical treatment, or enjoying the beauty God creates in nature, taking a moment to pray can provide a sense of grounding and clarity.

This mindful practice allows one to focus on gratitude, seek guidance, or find peace amidst chaos.

In these special times, prayer can serve as a bridge between the individual and something greater. This will foster a sense of connection to the universe or to loved ones, both present and absent. I find that it transforms fleeting moments into lasting memories. Moments that are infused with intension and reflection.

This makes each prayer not just a ritual or a request, but a heartfelt expression of one's innermost self.

Remember to do the following daily :

1) Put on your "Happy Soxx" and start your day with a smile
2) Wear Color because "Cancer Hates Color"
3) Be a Positive Spirit by being in the present - offer prayer
4) Get to know and respect your caregivers
5) Try to add humor were appropriate
6) Get in touch with family and friends - great elements of support
7) Everyone has challenges - it's how we deal with them that matters

www.ingramcontent.com/pod-product-compliance
Lightning Source LLC
Chambersburg PA
CBHW040846120626
46547CB00001B/44